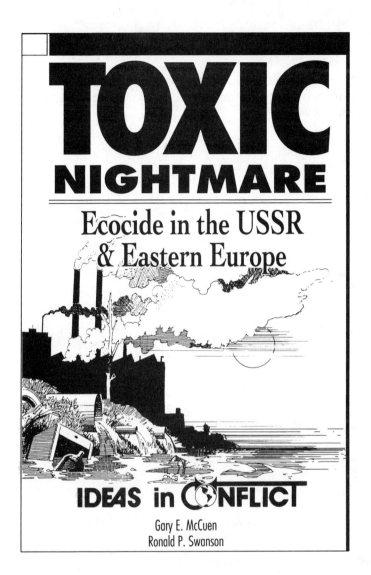

TOXIC NIGHTMARE

Ecocide in the USSR & Eastern Europe

IDEAS in CONFLICT

Gary E. McCuen
Ronald P. Swanson

GEM
GARY McCUEN
publications inc.

411 Mallalieu Drive
Hudson, Wisconsin 54016
Phone (715) 386-7113

Illustrations & Photo Credits

Bill Sanders 103 Jerry Fearing 20 Karl Markusen - Greenpeace, Germany 59 Ron Swanson 12, 34, 45, 53, 66, 84, 97, 107, 113

© 1993 By Gary E. McCuen Publications, Inc.
411 Mallalieu Drive, Hudson, Wisconsin 54016

(715) 386-7113

International Standard Book Number
0-86596-090-9 Printed in the United States
of America

CONTENTS

Ideas in Conflict

CHAPTER 3 REVERSING THE TREND: IDEAS IN CONFLICT

REASONING SKILL DEVELOPMENT

The following activities may be used as individualized study guides for students in libraries and resource centers or as discussion catalysts in small group and classroom discussions.

IDEAS in CONFLICT

This series features ideas in conflict on political, social, and moral issues. It presents counterpoints, debates, opinions, commentary, and analysis for use in libraries and classrooms. Each title in the series uses one or more of the following basic elements:

Introductions *that present an issue overview giving historic background and/or a description of the controversy.*

Counterpoints *and debates carefully chosen from publications, books, and position papers on the political right and left to help librarians and teachers respond to requests that treatment of public issues be fair and balanced.*

Symposiums *and forums that go beyond debates that can polarize and oversimplify. These present commentary from across the political spectrum that reflect how complex issues attract many shades of opinion.*

A **global** *emphasis with foreign perspectives and surveys on various moral questions and political issues that will help readers to place subject matter in a less culture-bound and ethnocentric frame of reference. In an ever-shrinking and interdependent world, understanding and cooperation are essential. Many issues are global in nature and can be effectively dealt with only by common efforts and international understanding.*

Reasoning skill *study guides and discussion activities provide ready-made tools for helping with critical reading and evaluation of content. The guides and activities deal with one or more of the following:*

RECOGNIZING AUTHOR'S POINT OF VIEW

INTERPRETING EDITORIAL CARTOONS

VALUES IN CONFLICT

WHAT IS EDITORIAL BIAS?

WHAT IS SEX BIAS?

WHAT IS POLITICAL BIAS?

WHAT IS ETHNOCENTRIC BIAS?

WHAT IS RACE BIAS?

WHAT IS RELIGIOUS BIAS?

*From across **the political spectrum** varied sources are presented for research projects and classroom discussions. Diverse opinions in the series come from magazines, newspapers, syndicated columnists, books, political speeches, foreign nations, and position papers by corporations and nonprofit institutions.*

About the Editor

Gary E. McCuen is an editor and publisher of anthologies for public libraries and curriculum materials for schools. Over the past years his publications have specialized in social, moral and political conflict. They include books, pamphlets, cassettes, tabloids, filmstrips and simulation games, many of them designed from his curriculums during 11 years of teaching junior and senior high school social studies. At present he is the editor and publisher of the *Ideas in Conflict* series and the *Editorial Forum* series.

CHAPTER 1

ENVIRONMENTAL DEVASTATION IN THE SOVIET UNION

1 ENVIRONMENTAL DEVASTATION IN THE SOVIET UNION

POLLUTION'S HAVOC IS CLEAR – SOLUTIONS ARE NOT

Frank Wright

Frank Wright is a foreign correspondent for the Minneapolis-based Star Tribune.

Points to Consider:

1. What is happening to the town of Zaporozhye?

2. Why is so little being done to change things?

3. What are the health costs of pollution in the USSR?

4. Who is the "third angel"?

Frank Wright, "Pollution's Havoc Is Clear; Solutions Are Not," **Star Tribune**, October 13, 1991. Reprinted with permission of the **Star Tribune**.

Medieval cities are blackened and crumbling. Whole hillsides are deforested. Almost 20 percent of water samples fail to meet health standards.

Hariy Kalayada, research director at a huge electrical transformer factory, knows his Bible. Especially Revelation, the book of the Apocalypse.

The Bible, however, gives little comfort to him and his neighbors in Zaporozhye. An industrial city of almost a million people in eastern Ukraine, it is perhaps the worst among the scores of Stalin-era environmental atrocities that have come to light since the fall of communism opened Eastern Europe and the (former) Soviet Union to closer inspection.

To clean up Zaporozhye and other catastrophes like it throughout the old Communist bloc will take billions of dollars that the (former) Soviet Union and its past satellites don't have and that the West is unwilling to provide. Clamping down on the rampant pollution also risks the elimination of countless jobs, a fate that makes even environmentalists tremble, given the fragility of the economies.

Not to clean up the Zaporozhyes, on the other hand, potentially dooms thousands to early deaths as well as condemning the atmosphere, the Earth and its waters.

To Kalayada, the story of Revelation's third angel comes uncomfortably close to home. He considers it the horrendous tale of Chernobyl, 300 miles to the northwest, where an atomic reactor exploded in April 1986, contaminating the air, the rain, the earth and the rivers of the Ukraine and adjacent republics with nuclear fallout that has killed thousands and sickened many more, with the final toll to be known only years in the future.

Kalayada fears the story of the fourth angel may become the story of his own Zaporozhye, a city that embodies the Stalinist idea of nature as a resource to be ruthlessly exploited.

Factory smoke and toxic plumes regularly blot the sky. Chemical and coal fumes fill the lungs around the clock. Industrial and human wastes flow continuously into the Dnieper River. Together with farm runoff, they have turned the Dnieper, the 1,400-mile lifeline that runs past Chernobyl, Kiev and Zaporozhye, into an open sewer on its way to the Black Sea.

The Old Guard

Not many outsiders have heard of Zaporozhye despite its size and its history that goes back centuries. It was the heart of fierce Cossack resistance to Tatars, Turks, Poles and others who would encroach on their freedom, succumbing only after a 1654 treaty gave Peter the Great control of most of the Ukraine and helped him launch the Russian Empire.

Iron ore is mined nearby, and steel mills are the city's core. Railway equipment factories, metallurgical workshops, refineries, potash-processing plants and military arsenals are clustered throughout the city. None is equipped with pollution-control devices. Jobs numbering well into the tens of thousands depend on the smoke stacks.

Despite the collapse in Moscow of the attempted coup by hardline Communists, Zaporozhye is one of those many provincial outposts where the old guard continues to dominate the local government. "We can get nothing done," said Kalayada, a leader of the democratic opposition and an environmental advocate. Many factory directors and warehouse managers also are members of the county and city councils, enabling them to sit in judgment on pollution-control proposals. The proposals get nowhere.

A rare demonstration against pollution was organized in August of 1991. Instigated by university students from Moscow, the protesters began a hunger strike in the city square. They demanded that the local government implement new laws requiring that the smelters either install cleanup devices or shut down.

SOVIET

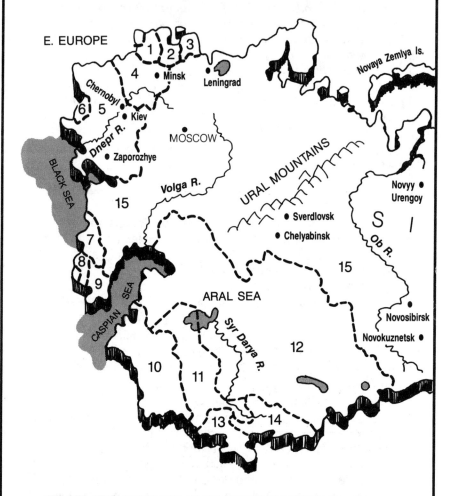

E. EUROPE

Novaya Zemlya Is.

1 2 3

4 • Minsk
• Leningrad

Chernobyl

6 5 • Kiev

Dnepr R.

MOSCOW

• Zaporozhye

BLACK SEA

Volga R.

15

URAL MOUNTAINS

Novyy •
Urengoy

S |

• Sverdlovsk
• Chelyabinsk

Ob R.

7

8

9

CASPIAN SEA

ARAL SEA

Syr Darya R.

15

• Novosibirsk

Novokuznetsk •

10 11 12

13 14

THE FORMER SOVIET REPUBLICS

ARMENIA	KAZAKHSTAN	RUSSIA
AZERBAIJAN	KIRGHIZIA	TAJIKISTAN
BYELORUSSIA	LATVIA	TURKMENISTAN
ESTONIA	LITHUANIA	UKRAINE
GEORGIA	MOLDAVIA	UZBEKISTAN

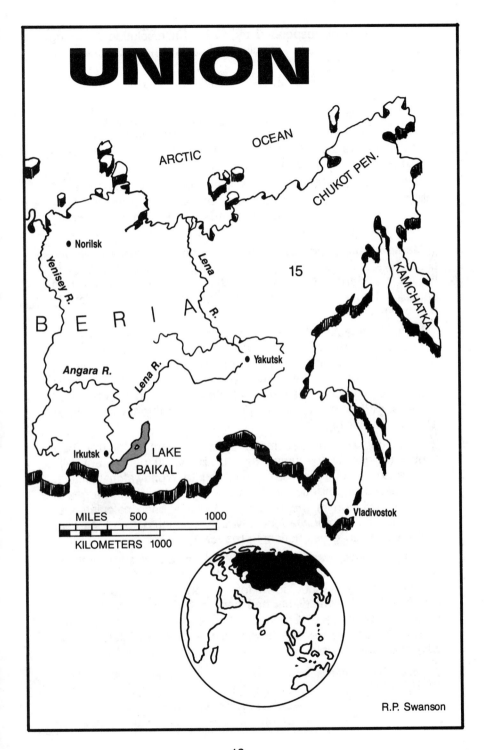

UNION

ARCTIC OCEAN

CHUKOT PEN.

● Norilsk

Yenisey R.

Lena

B E R I A

R.

KAMCHATKA

15

Angara R.

Lena R.

● Yakutsk

Irkutsk ●

LAKE
BAIKAL

● Vladivostok

MILES 500 1000

KILOMETERS 1000

R.P. Swanson

The city council responded by passing a resolution declaring it bore no responsibility for pollution and had no authority to do anything about it.

A Nightmare

Not until 1989 did the Soviet government release its first report on the national environment, a report detailing alarming pollution of the air and water, rapidly spreading environmental health problems and degradation of soil and forest.

In more than 100 cities, with a population of more than 50 million, Soviet air-pollution standards are exceeding tenfold. Only 30 percent of Soviet sewage is adequately treated. Twenty percent is dumped raw.

Medieval cities are blackened and crumbling. Whole hillsides are deforested. Almost 20 percent of water samples fail to meet health standards. At least 1.5 billion tons of topsoil erode annually. Two-thirds of the country's arable land has lost fertility due to erosion.

Largely because of the polluted Dnieper, 90 percent of the Black Sea is biologically dead. Resorts are imperiled and beaches closed along the shores of both the Black and Caspian Seas. Fish harvests have dropped by two-thirds. In the worst areas, life expectancies are years lower than in less-polluted regions. Rates of cancer, reproductive problems and other ailments are far higher.

Pesticide concentrates make up to 30 percent of the food supply dangerous to human health, kill 14,000 people annually and cause 700,000 illnesses, according to Worldwatch Institute, a U.S.-based organization that monitors global issues. The health costs of pollution in the Soviet Union have been calculated at more than $300 billion annually which amounted to 10 percent of the estimated gross national product.

Some progress was being made. (Former) Soviet environmental standards tended to be higher than those in the West. In 1989, 240 factories were shut down for environmental reasons. Plans for 30 nuclear power plants had been abandoned or suspended indefinitely because of Chernobyl. But, overall, enforcement was lax. As in Zaporozhye, the government and the polluters usually were the same people.

Little Power

The plight of Yuri Scherbak is an example of how environmental protection in the Soviet Union was not always what it appeared to be. He won election to the Ukrainian parliament as a member of the anti-Communist opposition. When the Communist majority offered to make him the republic's first minister of environmental protection, he accepted although he knew the offer was a bribe. "They want the appearance of a unified government, which is not the fact," Scherbak said.

His first act was largely symbolic. He took down the portrait of Lenin that adorned his new office and put in its place a portrait of V.I. Vernadsky, an early Ukrainian environmental scientist who was executed on Stalin's orders. Approximately 100 environmental laws were passed by the republic parliament in 1990. In July, the ministry for the first time was granted authority to fine violators.

But Scherbak had few resources—only two lawyers—and little real enforcement power as long as the former Communists remained in control and government-run enterprises were the main employers as well as the major polluters.

Nevertheless, he was serious about the job and said he wanted to do the best he could in order to build a record of good intentions that would help the opposition in the Ukraine. He said he would bring as many cases as he could against violators. The potential appeared unlimited. The Ukraine, Scherbak said, has only 3 percent of the land area of the Soviet Union but, because of its extensive agriculture, mining and heavy industry, produces 25 percent of the pollutants.

Standing before a huge wall map in his Kiev office, he pointed out what he and other environmentalists regarded as one environmental disaster after another. In Cerkassy, a chemical-processing city downriver from Kiev, 20 percent of the children are born with severe physical defects. In Cernovcy, a

15

thallium-and boron-producing city of 300,000 in western Ukraine, several thousand children, most of them blondes, have become bald. This unexplained phenomenon is also appearing elsewhere. The list goes on, seemingly without end.

The Third Angel

The news about Chernobyl seems only to get worse. The conclusion that the tragedy was of far greater magnitude than originally described is firmly imbedded in the minds of the Soviet public and much of the scientific and medical community.

There is now evidence, for instance, that:

- Children were especially vulnerable to the fallout, as measured by higher-than-normal rates of thyroid problems, anemia, cancer, leukemia and other maladies. To mention two specificis, Thyroid problems doubled in southern Byelorussia, and anemia in the fallout zone increased up to 800 percent.

- While the number of immediate Chernobyl deaths still is listed at 31, some Soviet officials say it may have been as high as 7,000.

- In the Ukraine alone, 12.5 million acres of farmland and almost 4 million acres of forest are radioactively contaminated.

Almost everyone has his own story, prompting the public to discredit widely a report by the International Atomic Energy Agency declaring that much of the (former) Soviet people's concern is based on psychological trauma rather than on real physical problems caused by the explosion.

One of those stories is from Boris Tymoschenko, a Ukrainian writer with whom I stayed for a week in August. He had room in his apartment in Kiev because his wife was in the United States, overseeing a planeload of Ukrainian children who were being treated for what were considered Chernobyl-related ailments.

In addition, the Tymoschenkos had room because their two sons are semi-permanently in the States for treatment. One, now in his early 20s, is suffering from a rare blood disorder believed to have been caused when he and thousands of other Kiev youngsters were caught in a radioactive rain carried to Kiev from Chernobyl, during a May Day parade five days after the explosion.

Authorities had made no announcement of the explosion, and the general public had no knowledge of it. The other son, now in his early teens, suddenly stopped growing after the explosion and fallout.

Another tale comes from Peter Ivanovich Livshan, a driver who worked for 10 days at Chernobyl as a volunteer two months after the reactor blew apart. Livshan repeatedly drove a concrete truck directly onto the explosion site and dropped his load into the reactor as part of the effort to seal it in a huge sarcophagus.

He said five members of the squad of 30 men with whom he worked now suffer from blood disorders. As for himself, he said, his only problem is what he calls an unexplained fungus that grows in his mouth from time to time. What reward did he get for volunteering? He proudly displays an official document that he says will permit him to retire 10 years early, at age 50.

"If I and my fungus live that long."

2 ENVIRONMENTAL DEVASTATION IN THE SOVIET UNION

SIBERIA: TROUBLE ON THE FRONTIER

Mike Edwards

Mike Edwards is a senior staff writer for the National Geographic Magazine. *In this article, Edwards reports on the environmental degradation he witnessed on his journey across Siberia.*

Points to Consider:

1. Who are the Nentsy and where do they live?

2. How are they being threatened?

3. What was the "period of stagnation"?

4. Briefly describe the appearance of a typical Siberian city.

5. What will happen to Siberia now that the former Soviet Union has broken up?

Mike Edwards, "Siberia: In from the Cold," **National Geographic Magazine**, March 1990.

Rivers are spoiled, wildlife is disappearing, the air is foul with the stench of sulfur and the tundra is becoming a toxic waste dump.

The deeper I went into Siberia, the more I encountered the "period of stagnation", the term applied to the 18-year regime (1964-1982) of the late Soviet President Leonid Brezhnev. Anything that's wrong, BIOB: Blame It On Brezhnev. As former President Gorbachev sought to inspire *perestroika*, (new methods) he excoriated his predecessor, and bureaucrats took up the cry.

Stagnation denied citizens improved housing and other comforts. But in development this was an era, as the Soviets say, of *gigantomaniya*. Billions of rubles were invested in huge Siberian dams, mines, mills — the bigger, the better — with scant regard for the environment. At Bratsk, 750 miles east of Novosibirsk, rose a great dam, then a great aluminum smelter to utilize its electricity. And nearby a pulp mill so large it still can't secure wood enough to run at capacity. Bratsk is reportedly among Siberia's most polluted cities. Local party officials didn't approve my request to visit — because, I believe, they didn't want me to see the environmental mess.

While building big, Brezhnev gave little thought to cleaning up existing industry. This is demonstrated in the Kuzbas, "the valley of a thousand smokes".

It's only a Siberian hop-skip — about 200 miles — from Novosibirsk southeast to the heart of this coal-mining basin, the city of Novokuznetsk. I took an overnight train on a spur of the Trans-Siberian. A sleepless trip: we stopped at a dozen villages and were rattled every few minutes by passing coal trains rolling out of the Kuzbas.

In winter the air may be as still as death over Novokuznetsk. Pollutants linger. I went to the local *Goskompriroda* (the Soviet equivalent of the U.S. Environmental Protection Agency) office to ask about the effects. A scientist alluded vaguely to health problems among the 600,000 citizens. Asked to elaborate, he hesitated, glancing at his colleagues; this was their first encounter with a Western journalist. Finally, he plunged on: lung cancer rates are 30 percent higher than the average for Soviet industrial cities, and respiratory infections and eye inflammations among children are higher. Industrial dust and sulfur dioxide are blamed.

Near that office is the huge Kuznetsky Metallurgical Kombinat

(KMK) steelworks, a symbol of Soviet might. Men with shovels and wheelbarrows built this mill in the 1930s as Joseph Stalin strove to industrialize. The city grew up beside it. Workers proudly claim that in World War II KMK armored half of all Soviet tanks.

It was a rude surprise for KMK's director, Aleksei Kuznetsov, to see protesters in front of his headquarters one day. "I am being ruthlessly criticized," said Kuznetsov, a bluff man with graying hair. Goskompriroda is peppering him with hundred-ruble fines and trying to block his bonus until KMK is cleaned up.

Responding to demands from city officials and citizens, KMK has closed some of its works, including two coking ovens that sent up sulfur and nitrogen compounds. But fires still roar in 14 furnaces in the cavernous building that poured tank armor. The fumes and dust are choking.

An Exceptional Country

"The (former) Soviet Union is an exceptional country," declared Gennadi Filshin, an economist. "Exceptions were given to build a lot of polluting enterprises." His sarcasm emphasized the "Swiss cheese" enforcement of a law banning environmentally damaging factories.

Nearly as big as Texas and Louisiana combined, Irkutsk Oblast (region) is heavily industrialized, producing aluminum, chemicals, and wood pulp. In nearby Angarsk, a thousand choking citizens went to hospitals when a plant producing animal-feed supplements vented a heavy dose of protein particles.

Irkutsk citizens march to protest pollution and stridently demand that Moscow let them share in developing decisions.

Norilsk welcomed me hospitably, with memorable feasts, as if there had never been a Cold War—and as if Norilsk were not a source of militarily strategic metals. I found people invariably proud that they'd accommodated to the hostile environment. Many have lived here a dozen years or more. Yelena Kalininskaya, for one. Tough, enterprising Yelena could run General Motors, but in Norilsk she bosses the local farm, providing milk from a herd of cows as well as cucumbers and onions from greenhouses. She's one reason life is tolerable for 175,000 people.

Ores were discovered here in the 1920s. Stalin sent political prisoners to mine and build. Thousands died. After the forced labor camps were closed in the 1950s, paid workers continued to develop the mine-smelter complex. It is dirty—deadening rivers with effluent, raining sulfuric acid on the tundra.

The smelters' high stacks are supposed to waft away sulfurous smoke. But on windless days Norilsk smells like hellfire, and the smelters have to cut back operations.

The Endless Frontier [1]

Siberia, according to some accounts, originally meant "sleeping giant". A glance eastward toward the giant land mass beyond the Ural Mountains of northern Asia will quickly convince you that, today, this is rapidly changing. Helicopters are laying pipeline, chainsaws are slicing the forests and huge factories

1 The following material was paraphrased by the editors from Mike Edward's article cited previously on page 18.

RUSSIA'S FORGOTTEN LANDS

Atmospheric nuclear bomb tests conducted at numerous sites across the Soviet Far North during the 1950s and 1960s have contaminated the entire food chain from Murmansk in the west to the Chukot Peninsula on the shores of the Bering Strait. In our scientific investigations, we found that in these regions the total radioactive dose was double the average for the rest of the USSR and concentrations of cesium-137 in the native population were 100 times higher than normal.

Vladimir M. Lupandin, "Russia's Forgotten Lands," **Earth Island Journal**, Fall 1991.

belch pollutants into the air as development invades the "frontier".

Siberian cities are dirty cities, Novosibirsk and Irkutsk being among the former Soviet Union's 70 most polluted. Novosibirsk, located some 1,800 miles east of Moscow, became the site of steel and heavy machine production during World War II. Industry continued to develop here, and today the residents must contend with foul air and wastewater loaded with dangerous chemicals. Other Siberian cities share this fate, as the region's rich deposits of oil, natural gas, coal, gold and iron are increasingly exploited.

Getting around in Siberia and Russia's Far East is no small task. More than one fourth of the continent of Asia, it is larger than the U.S. and Mexico combined. It is so vast that Americans living in the state of Maine are closer to Moscow than are Russians living in the most distant towns of the region. It takes nearly eleven hours of flying time, covering eleven time zones, to span the 6,200 mile journey from Moscow to the east. Somewhat rectangular in shape, it measures over 2,000 miles from north to south and extends nearly 4,000 miles from the Urals to the Pacific Ocean in the Far East.

Siberia's six million square miles are contained in what is now the independent Russian Republic. The population is well over 30 million including sizeable native populations widely dispersed throughout the region. Geographically, Siberia consists of three distinct climatic zones. The tundra, in the north, is a treeless area of frozen ground (permafrost) extending hundreds of miles south from the Arctic. Winters are brutal and summers are short. Agriculture is impossible here, but the land suits the reindeer and other wildlife. The taiga zone is dominated by forest-covered lowlands of spruce, fir, pine, larch, birch, aspen and cedar. This dense growth of trees will surely be a prime target of development for the Russian Republic as it switches to a market economy. To the south lies the steppe, a level grassland blessed with fertile soils for agriculture and an abundance of natural resources. Throughout their history, Russians have always been close to the land. Today, that land is threatened with the specter of environmental destruction.

The Dead Lake

In the midst of bogs and wandering rivers near Niznevartovsk is Lake Samotlor, or "dead lake", in the language of the local Khanty people. When the first oil wells were sunk here in 1969, the local economy boomed. Today, the Samotlor Field still delivers some 780 million barrels a year, the highest production in the world. But according to environmentalists, millions of barrels are spilled into local streams and threaten the fishing communities of the area. Sturgeon populations are affected downstream along the Ob, one of Siberia's major rivers, as the heavy oil settles on the bottom where the sturgeon feed. Heavy metals, pesticides and human waste add to the terrible problems of the Ob, probably the most polluted river in Russia.

Further to the north, the town of Novyy (New) Urengoy became a center of natural gas production during the Brezhnev years. Power lines and roads criss-cross the delicate tundra. 1,400 wells produce 14 trillion cubic feet of gas each year. The crash program of development has taken its toll on the land. Rivers are spoiled, wildlife is disappearing, the air is foul with the stench of sulfur, and the tundra is becoming a toxic waste dump.

The Indigenous Fight Back

For the Nentsy, the Evenk and other indigenous groups, the environmental devastation in Siberia really hits home — a home they have called their own for thousands of years. Energy is a big concern in Russia today, and as demand grows, the oil and gas of Siberia will be increasingly exploited. The Nentsy fear what this development will do to their way of life. Herding reindeer has been their livelihood in the frozen north. The Nentsy and other groups lost much of their leadership when Stalin had them shipped off to labor camps in the 1930s. The Soviet

CHERNOBYL WASN'T FIRST

In the late '40s, the first Soviet nuclear reactor for the production of weapon-grade plutonium was commissioned in a place a hundred kilometers outside Chelyabinsk. The plutonium went to fill the bombs, and the waste was dumped into the Techa River.

In the fall of 1957, one of Mayak's waste capacities blew up, venting into the air an equivalent of almost half the Chernobyl dose. The resulting radioactive cloud covered an area of 23,000 square kilometers containing 217 villages and 270,000 people.

Waste containing the radioactive equivalent of two and a half Chernobyls has been dumped into Lake Karachia seeping into the water table below (which can at any time burst into the Ob River tributaries.)

There are another 200 burials of 500,000 tons of solid waste, and half a billion cubic meters of contaminated water in a group of artificial ponds in the upper reaches of the Techa, and these will start spilling over in another year or two.

Andrei Borodenkov, "Chernobyl Wasn't the First!" **Moscow News**, 1991,

government showed little concern for the Nentsy as the helicopters brought in geologists with tundra-ripping tractor vehicles, and construction began on railroads, docks, houses, roads, drilling pads, electric power stations and other facilities necessary for oil and gas production. But the Nentsy have recently won support among environmentalists and have even halted a massive development project in the Yamal Peninsula.

Other indigenous groups have suffered as well — the Buryat of the Lake Baikal region north of Mongolia lost 10,000 of their people to Stalin's purges and nearly all their Buddhist temples. The Evenk in the north, numbering only 4,000, have watched as the newcomers have gobbled up their reindeer pastures, poisoned their streams and poached their wildlife. Despite some minor victories, these indigenous people cannot stop the inevitable — their efforts must concentrate on promoting conservation and wise land-use policies to a Russian Republic eager to develop its natural resources.

Goskompriroda, the Soviet equivalent of the U.S. Environmental Protection Agency, was created in 1988 to deal with the enforcement of laws regulating polluters. From the start, the agency lacked any real clout. Tougher rules were always opposed by the manufacturing and extracting ministries. Under perestroika, many industries underwent "self-financing" measures meant to ease central control and begin the change-over to a free market economy. New equipment including pollution-control devices were to be purchased from the profits. For many factories including the KMK of Kuznetsky, this was unrealistic. One alternative was to simply close the plant down. This, however, is also unrealistic considering the economic climate of the post-Soviet era.

As the Russian Republic develops its own free-market economy, Siberia will become its main supplier of natural resources. Japanese and U.S. investors are already looking to the vast forests of the taiga as a supply of lumber and other wood products. With tremendous reserves of oil, natural gas and minerals, Siberia will continue to be exploited as Russia's primary source of exports. Unless past policies of environmental destruction are reversed, this vast and seemingly endless frontier will soon become the largest toxic waste dump on earth.

3 ENVIRONMENTAL DEVASTATION IN THE SOVIET UNION

LAKE BAIKAL INSPIRES RUSSIAN CLEAN-UP EFFORT

Michael Dobbs

Michael Dobbs wrote this article for the Washington Post. *The article deals with the efforts to clean up the ecological problems of Lake Baikal in Siberia.*

Points to Consider:

1. What is the pulp mill at Baikalsk doing to the lake?

2. How does Lake Baikal symbolize the ecological problems in Siberia?

3. What effect does the Angarsk chemical plant have on the Baikal area?

4. How has the life expectancy changed in Russia? Why has this change taken place?

The ecological threat to Lake Baikal has developed within the lifespan of a single generation.

"Make Effective Use of the Natural Resources of Siberia!" proclaimed the faded propaganda board by the side of this mile-deep lake that contains one-fifth of the world's freshwater supply.

Nearby, a pile of white marble mined from the mountains that rise up around Baikal was lying abandoned. About 15 miles away, across the translucent waters of the beautiful inland sea, a cellulose plant was pumping black clouds into the blue sky. On the other side of the lake, dozens of factories around the city of Ulan-Ude were releasing chemical pollutants into the Selenga River, which provides Baikal with half its water.

"Nobody bothers to think about these slogans, what they mean or how to implement them," said Vadim Firsov, an inspector of a new environmental watchdog agency. "They just sit in their offices, dreaming up anything. No wonder things are going badly."

"The idea of Russian sovereignty originated with the destruction of our environment and the plundering of Russia's resources," said Gennadi Filshin, the newly elected deputy prime minister of Russia, whose political career began with the campaign to save Lake Baikal. "The efficient use of resources is possible only when a real master of those resources appears. As long as decisions affecting the future of Siberia were made by some bureaucrat in Moscow, mismanagement was inevitable."

Growing Concerns

The greening of Russian public opinion has been particularly evident in Siberia, the source of most of the Soviet Union's oil, timber and hydroelectric energy. For centuries, Siberia was regarded as a land of virtually unlimited natural resources and endless spaces. The Siberian treasure house enabled the Soviet Union to become a global superpower. Over the past few years, many Russians have begun to understand that Siberia's wealth is limited and needs careful husbanding if future generations are to benefit.

Pollution is no worse in Siberia than in other parts of the (former) Soviet Union—and in remote regions, considerably less. What makes the situation particularly dramatic, however, is that the process of industrialization has been violently compressed. Vast areas of taiga, or northern coniferous forest, have been torn

27

A Nerpa, the world's only fresh-water seal, at home in Lake Baikal.

apart to make way for cities and industrial complexes. The ecological threat to Lake Baikal, which is at least 25 million years old and is home to 2,000 different plants and animals found nowhere else in the world, has developed within the lifespan of a single generation.

"Nature is taking its revenge," said Grigory Galazi, a marine biologist who has been at the forefront of the campaign to save Baikal, predicting that the clean-up of the lake will take many decades. "Nature is bountiful. She gives loans very easily. But she also charges interest on these loans that far exceed the original capital. It's taken a long time for us to realize this."

Multiple Threats

For many activists, the pulp-paper factory at Baikalsk has become a test case of the willingness of Russia's new government to take tough measures to protect the environment. Situated at the southern tip of the lake, it is the only major industrial enterprise on Baikal. A 1987 Kremlin decree ordered its closing or transformation into an ecologically harmless furniture factory by 1993. But there is no sign of this happening.

The pulp mill was built in the early 1960s, in the middle of the headlong dash toward the industrialization of Siberia. At the time, environmental issues were of little concern to Soviet leaders. There were practically no outlets for the expression of independent public opinion. In order to make the Soviet Union a global superpower and to catch up with the United States, industrial production had to be increased, whatever the cost.

The Ministry of Forestry Industry argued that the pure water of Lake Baikal was needed to produce super cellulose cord for aircraft tires. In order to produce one ton of pulp, 375 tons of fresh water and about 500 pounds of sodium sulfate (much more than in Western countries) are required. The filthy wastes are purified but, even so, the water pumped back into the lake is considerably less pure than the water extracted a few miles away. It also has a slightly unpleasant odor.

The managers of the pulp plant insist that their opponents have not been able to produce hard evidence that the factory constitutes a serious ecological threat to Baikal. They also are dismayed at the burst of negative publicity their factory has been receiving in Russian newspapers, which have become much more sensitive to environmental controversies.

"We are depicted as irresponsible polluters. But we love Baikal as much as anyone," said Viktor Kostigin, the deputy director of the plant. "Our new media have begun to blacken everything and everyone. A few years ago, they said that everything was wonderful in the Soviet Union. Now they say that everything is terrible."

The environmentalists claim that the pulp plant is far from being the only threat to Baikal. Sewage and industrial wastes from Ulan-Ude, the construction of a new railroad along the northern shores of the lake, and air pollution from the industrial cities around Irkutsk all have exacted their toll. They question the need for a huge industrial complex right next to a lake that is as much a part of Russia's natural heritage as the Grand Canyon is of America's.

The marine and plant life of Baikal already has suffered as a result of the cumulative effects of pollution. The omul, a slender, salmon-like fish native to Baikal, has lost half its average weight over the past two decades. Its traditional spawning grounds in the estuary of the Selenga have been covered by sunken logs. The nerpa, the world's only fresh-water seal, also could be endangered if industrialization continues at its present rate.

"By destroying Baikal, we are destroying the basis of our own life," biologist Galazi said. "Human beings are themselves 60

29

percent water. Life first appeared in water—pure water, not water that has first gone through a pulp plant."

The uniqueness of Baikal was underlined in the summer of 1990 when a team of Soviet and U.S. scientists announced that they had discovered a field of hot-air vents at the bottom of the lake. The vents, which support a rich variety of life in the lake, are the first such formations to be found in fresh water. The scientists say that the scimitar-shaped lake could develop into an infant ocean as Asia splits apart.

The Angarsk Chemical Plant

From the balcony of his home in Angarsk, about 60 miles northwest of Baikal, the newly elected president of the regional environment protection committee has a grandstand view of a chemical plant. The plant produces almost as much airvorne pollution as the whole of Moscow, which has been declared an environmental crisis area.

"This is why I became interested in the environment," said Ildus Gapyautdinov, pointing at the clouds of noxious black smoke spewing out of the chemical plant. "For 73 years, we have had a policy of exploiting our resources without caring about future generations. It's not until there was a crisis that people began to stop and think."

The prevailing winds usually disperse the pollution from the Angarsk chemical plant over Baikal. But sometimes, when the winds are in the wrong direction, it floats back over Angarsk, a typical Stalin-era industrial city of workers' apartment blocks and grandiose public buildings. Local residents complain that breathing becomes more difficult and that the rain contains a corrosive acid.

It is difficult to calculate how much damage the Angarsk plant does to public health. But across Russia, the shocking effects of environmental neglect are evident. Russia is one of the few places in the world where life expectancy has fallen over the past decade. It is now down to an average of 65 years, eight to 10 years lower than in most industrialized countries. Every second Russian called up for military service is declared to be physically unfit.

According to official statistics, ecological crisis zones cover about 16 percent of Soviet territory. Between 50 million and 70 million people live in regions officially described as "ecologically unhealthy". Baikal is officially classified as a "crisis zone", one notch down from a "catastrophic zone", meaning that it will take decades for the environment to recover, even under the most favorable circumstances.

4 ENVIRONMENTAL DEVASTATION IN THE SOVIET UNION

CHERNOBYL: LIFE UNDER A DEADLY CLOUD

Rebecca Laird

Rebecca Laird is a free-lance writer and editor based in San Francisco. She has traveled to Byelorussia with Citihope, a San Francisco-based religious charity that works with the Byelorussian Children's Fund.

Points to Consider:

1. How many people have been affected by the Chernobyl disaster?

2. How many have been evacuated?

3. Why are crops still being grown in contaminated soil?

4. What is the fate of those residents who do not leave?

In Minsk, the sickest children of the contaminated regions are gathered in sparse, ill-equipped hospitals. Dozens of bald-headed chemotherapy patients line the wards.

On April 26, 1986, one of the four reactors at the Chernobyl nuclear power station exploded. Silence blanketed the world for three days while radioactive particles fell to the earth from the deadly cloud. Geiger counters and dosimeters (hand-held geiger counters) throughout Eastern Europe began to register the horrifying increase in radioactivity as the winds spread the invisible isotopes far and wide.

The Soviet Union could no longer keep this disaster quiet, and the news wires began to clatter—our worst nightmare had come true. The explosion produced 90 times more radioactive fallout than the bomb dropped on Hiroshima, altering the world's biosphere forever.

Other news soon replaced Chernobyl in U.S. headlines, but for the people of Byelorussia, the Soviet republic just across the Pripyat River, the Chernobyl disaster remains a current event. The 2.2 million people who live in contaminated regions have altered their daily lives to deal with radiation. Digital clocks atop official buildings in Minsk, the capital city of Byelorussia, flash the time, temperature, and radiation level every few seconds.

Seventy percent of all the radioactive fallout fell on this region of 14 million people (20 percent fell on the Ukraine and 10 percent on other parts of the Soviet Union and Europe). Today, 173,000 Byelorussians, including 37,000 children, are being monitored for radiation sickness. The occurrence of thyroid, kidney, and general diseases has dramatically increased. Doctors report higher miscarriage rates in pregnant women and more birth defects in children born to parents living in contaminated areas. Exposure to high levels of radiation especially suppresses the immune systems of growing children. Even common colds can readily lead to chronic respiratory problems.

Life Goes On

In 1991, I traveled to Byelorussia as part of a relief delegation bringing three tons of medicine. Our journey took us into the contaminated regions where the people continue to work, learn, and love; yet the Chernobyl catastrophe lurks just below the surface of their everyday lives.

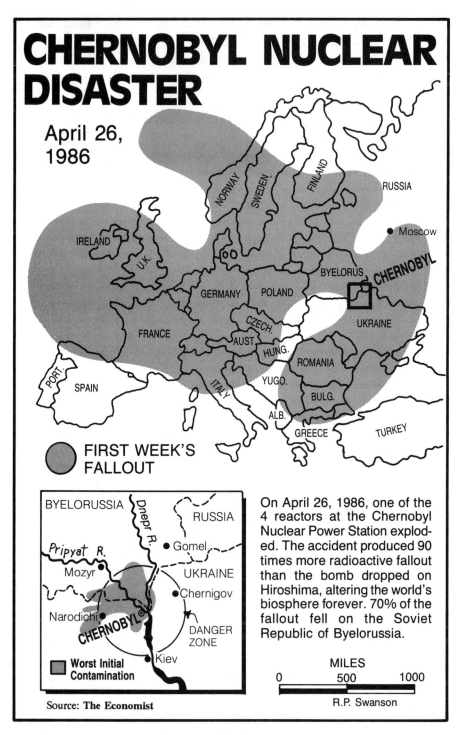

CHERNOBYL NUCLEAR DISASTER

April 26, 1986

RUSSIA

NORWAY

SWEDEN

FINLAND

Moscow

IRELAND

U.K.

BYELORUS

CHERNOBYL

GERMANY

POLAND

UKRAINE

CZECH.

AUST

FRANCE

HUNG.

ROMANIA

PORT.

SPAIN

ITALY

YUGO.

BULG.

ALB.

GREECE

TURKEY

FIRST WEEK'S FALLOUT

BYELORUSSIA

Dnepr R.

RUSSIA

Pripyat R.

Gomel

Mozyr

UKRAINE

Chernigov

Narodichi

CHERNOBYL

DANGER ZONE

Kiev

Worst Initial Contamination

On April 26, 1986, one of the 4 reactors at the Chernobyl Nuclear Power Station exploded. The accident produced 90 times more radioactive fallout than the bomb dropped on Hiroshima, altering the world's biosphere forever. 70% of the fallout fell on the Soviet Republic of Byelorussia.

MILES

0   500   1000

Source: The Economist

R.P. Swanson

Vitaliy Zheleznyak, a jowly man with bushy brows, is chair of the collective farm in the village of Vu Pokalybichi—once an enviable model of communal agrarian life. Vitaliy flashed his gold-capped smile as he boasted of the proud 60-year history of the 3,000-acre farm.

Today, this industrious collective continues to plant grain, potatoes, and wheat as well as roast Colombian-grown coffee beans. The problem is that nobody wants to buy the produce anymore. Soviet food shortages render the 1,200 cows too valuable to waste. Scientists insist the milk and meat register an "acceptable" level of radiation. The dairy products are shipped to various republics in the (former) Soviet Union, the attitude being that a little radiation spread among many is a lesser evil than hunger. The economic survival of the collective farm, as well as the entire region, requires that trade continue.

"Ideally," Vitaliy says, with the determination of one who is responsible for the welfare of 430 workers, "it would be better not to plant anything here. . .but taking into consideration our very poor economic situation, we must grow what we can with precautions and evaluations."

Vitaliy admits, "We don't feed our children with the food we grow because it is contaminated. We buy uncontaminated food from other regions. Still, 68 of our own children have been diagnosed with expanded thyroids and have experienced headaches and nose bleeds, the first signs of radiation sickness." The farm leaders coordinate an effort to send many of the area's 600 children away for the summers in hopes of restoring their immune systems.

Black Bitterness

Vitaliy remembers how it used to be—until April 26, 1986. "It was a beautiful, sunny, wonderful day until noon. About 4 p.m. my grandson and I saw a black cloud raining down what we didn't understand. So in such a way, in silence, being unaware of this accident, we were walking, enjoying our lives, not knowing of what was happening." Vitaliy is convinced that the forebears who named Chernobyl chose a prophetic name, for it means "black bitterness"—and that is what smolders beneath this thriving farm community.

Seventy kilometers from the Chernobyl reactor, Nikolai Markovski, a wiry, organized man in his mid-40s, sits at his desk and governs the Narovlia district, an area with triple the radiation level of the collective farm. Areas that register more than 15 curies of radiation are considered uninhabitable. On the day I

35

visited Narovlia, the air registered 37 curies. An old tree towers outside of Nikolai's office and spidery growths adorn the old limbs. "What kind of tree has limbs like that?" I asked, only to be told that what I saw were mutations caused by the radioactivity.

Twenty thousand people live in the Narovlia district. During the last five years, 8,000 people have been evacuated or moved to non-contaminated regions. Recent studies have shown that Narovlia is more contaminated than first thought. Eighty percent of those who now remain will be evacuated in the next year. All families with children under the age of 14 must leave. Families with older children can decide for themselves. Only eight of the original 40 villages in the district will be inhabited; the others will be deserted, left to decay.

Nikolai took me beyond the barbed wire where armed guards patrol the roads leading to the villages evacuated within weeks of the disaster. (Only four villages were actually bulldozed and buried). We drove to the border of Byelorussia and the Ukraine, just six kilometers from the nuclear reactor. Our dosimeter registered 366 curies in the air.

In the village of Dyornovichi, once home to 100 families, we walked through an abandoned kindergarten where toys, dolls,

VOICES FROM CHERNOBYL

Andrei Tormozini, Sasha Yushenko and Genady Ursanovsky were working at reactor number four the night it exploded. Evacuated to Moscow, they survived months of intensive care, repeated operations, blood transfusions and, in Andrei's case, a bone marrow transplant. They still suffer from chronic ailments and fatigue; their bodies are covered with radiation burns; they are frequently hospitalized and are too ill to work. They have been advised not to have children. The 31 of their co-workers who died at the reactor or in the Moscow hospital are still the only officially recognized fatalities from the accident.

There were more immediate victims. Over 600,000 so-called "liquidators" were brought in from all over the USSR to clean up the Chernobyl disaster. They wore cotton masks and stayed in dusty, heavily contaminated areas for weeks at a time, complaining of chronic flu-like symptoms: fatigue, headaches, fevers, rashes — typical radiation symptoms. Local medical staffs were ordered not to diagnose radiation illness.

James Lerager, "Voices from Chernobyl," **Earth Island Journal,** Spring 1991.

cots, and slippers had been strewn haphazardly around the room. Children played here for three full months after the disaster. Even after five years, hot spots around the facility registered 1,000 curies — one full rad — which is a lethal level of radiation when consistently exposed.

On the way back to Narovlia, Nikolai guided our driver past an evacuated village where several families have ignored governmental restrictions and moved back to their ancestral farms. An old, hunched woman walked out of her clapboard cottage to offer us fresh bread. She assured us that all of those who returned were well and happy. A couple of school-age girls ran across the road at her bidding.

Nikolai told us when we were back on the bus that many of the peasant farmers don't believe the radiation exists because it is invisible. Others acknowledge the presence of radiation, yet they could not adjust to life in the huge apartment complexes built for the refugees of the contaminated regions. They chose to return, knowing they might die young.

Nikolai is the father of an 11-year-old daughter and a 14-year-old son. When asked, "Will you leave?" he firmly shook his head and said, "The captain goes down with the ship. What about your children?" I asked. He shrugged sadly, "They know this is my job."

Playing with Nuclear Energy

Back in Minsk, the sickest children of the contaminated regions are gathered in sparse, ill-equipped hospitals. Dozens of bald-headed chemotherapy patients line the wards. The youngest ones posed eagerly for Polaroid pictures, which they then gave to their mothers who live at the hospital with them.

Four-year-old Andre Cochan and his mother have been at the Hematological Center in Minsk for four months. Andre, a bald bundle of energy dressed in a red and purple plaid shirt and blue wool pants, eagerly describes his life at home in the Borisov, 80 kilometers from Minsk. "I like to play with my dog and my cat, fish too. I have many small cars and in the summer there are flowers around my house." With a wide, expansive gesture, Andre, who longs to go home, declared, "Summer is coming—I can almost feel it on the tip of my nose."

Andre's father and grandfather care for Andre's baby brother in Borisov. Andre's greatest wish is that his papa would not have to work so that he could come to Minsk to play with him. When we bid him farewell, Andre nodded goodbye and wished us "good health and many years to live." Emotion choked in my throat as the leader of our delegation bent down and hugged him saying, "You, too, dear little one." I know my chances of a long life are so much greater than his.

"What do your people need most?" we asked the Minister of Health, Vaselli Karakov, when we met with him to determine priorities for the next shipment of medicine. "What we need most is help with the moral fortitude of the people. Their peace of mind has been destroyed. Souls are sick with despair. They need hope as well as medicines."

Minister Karakov went on to produce a long list of medical equipment and stressed the need for specialized training for the doctors. The medical professionals we met passionately care for the children yet they know that Western medicines and treatments could prolong the lives of 85 percent of the children.

Without training for the medical professionals and expensive medicines, most of the children will die simply because they played outside, ate the food of their land, and breathed the air. Such a price to pay for nuclear power.

Helen, one of the mothers at the collective farm, speaks for all of the Byelorussian people: "I lived earlier in the place, but I do not want to abandon the place of my birth. I'm not alone in this, so I stay. . . .We must not play with nuclear energy. Everybody wants a safe place to live."

Sadly, parts of Byelorussia will not be safe for generations to come.

READING THE DAILY NEWSPAPER

This activity may be used as an individualized study guide for students in libraries and resource centers or as a discussion catalyst in small group and classroom discussions.

One of the best sources for obtaining current information on social, political and environmental issues affecting our planet is the daily newspaper. The skill to read with insight and understanding involves the ability to know where to look and how to "skim" the headlines for articles of interest. The best place to begin is the front section and the opinion/editorial pages. Other good sources include the sections on the economy and any special feature sections that are usually included in Sunday editions. Be sure not to overlook the sections that deal with local issues as they often contain stories of global concern that are happening in your own community.

Guidelines

Using newspapers from home or from your school or local library, skim the headlines and locate articles that deal with ecology, Eastern Europe and the former Soviet Union. With the rapid changes taking place politically in these areas, today's headlines and editorials are a good source of information on the issues brought out in this book.

1. Try to locate several articles dealing with the topics of this chapter.

2. Do any of these articles or opinions discuss the ecological crisis in Eastern Europe or the former Soviet Union? If so, how do they relate to the readings in this book?

3. How might changes on the political scene affect the environment?

4. Do you believe that the emerging governments of the former Soviet Union will be able to deal effectively with the severe environmental problems? Why or why not? (Be sure to refer to your newspaper sources.)

5. Can you locate any articles or editorials that refute the content of any of the readings in this publication? If so, explain.

Other Projects

Start a scrapbook of articles, editorials and political cartoons dealing with environmental issues in Eastern Europe and the former Soviet Union. Prepare a short report or essay highlighting a story on a particular crisis or plan to reverse the damage. Be sure to include any maps or photos you may locate that illustrate the situation.

CHAPTER 2

EASTERN EUROPE: CAULDRON OF POISON

5

EASTERN EUROPE:
CAULDRON OF POISON

EUROPE'S INDUSTRIAL
WASTELAND

Hilary F. French

Hilary F. French researches international policy issues at the Worldwatch Institute. This article provides an overview of the terrible environmental damage in Eastern Europe. It was written before the fall of communism. Present environmental conditions, however, are still similar to the conditions described below.

Points to Consider:

1. What is the condition of Eastern Europe's drinking water?

2. Identify the chief source of air pollution in the region.

3. What is "Waldsterben"? How extensive is it?

4. How much of Poland's soil is too contaminated for agriculture?

Hilary F. French, "Industrial Wasteland," **Worldwatch,** November/December, 1988.

Centuries-old forests are being decimated. In four of the six Eastern European countries, a quarter to a third of the forests are showing signs of damage.

In Molbis, East Germany, the air pollution is so thick that drivers often have to turn on their headlights in the middle of the day. Revered monuments and artwork in the city of Krakow, Poland, are crumbling under the assault of air pollution and acid rain. Women with newborn babies in Czechoslovakia have priority access to bottled water because the tap water there is considered a hazard to infant health.

The Polish government has declared five villages in the industrial region of Silesia unfit to live in because of high levels of heavy metals in the soil. It has bought out most of the villagers, enabling them to relocate. In Czechoslovakia, residents aren't waiting for a formal decree: they're leaving heavily polluted northern Bohemia at such a rate that the government is offering them financial incentives to stay. Sources suggest that in Poland, Czechoslovakia and East Germany, in particular, industrial pollution has reached intolerable levels.

The problems faced by these countries are not unfamiliar to Westerners, who have also seen the condition of their air, land and water deteriorate. In the West, however, environmental protection has been on the agenda for nearly two decades; in the East, it is just beginning to emerge as a political issue.

Prodded by public pressure, several Eastern European nations appear to be recognizing the severity of their environmental crisis. However, it remains to be seen whether they will muster the political will and the economic resources to tackle it.

Tainted Water

In Eastern Europe, already one of the world's water-poor regions, water contamination is so severe that significant portions of those supplies that do exist are unfit for industrial use, let alone for drinking. Industrial waste—toxic chemicals, petroleum by-products, mine drainage and heavy metals—is a primary contributor to the problem, as are municipal sewage and agricultural run-off.

The rivers of the region are showing the effects of this abuse. Government officials estimate that 70 percent of the rivers flowing through Czechoslovakia are heavily polluted. The state-run radio reported in 1982 that more than 4,300 miles of river—28 percent of the nation's total—had no fish life.

EASTERN EUROPE

LATVIA

LITHUANIA · RUSSIA

Baltic Sea

BYELORUS

EAST

Gdansk

· Minsk

SILESIA

Vistula R.

Berlin

Espenhain

· Warsaw

GERMANY

Elbe R.

POLAND

BOHEMIA

· Katowice

Chernobyl ·

Prague

· Krakow

Kiev ·

Danube R.

CZECHOSLOVAKIA

UKRAINE

BAVARIA

MOLDAVIA

AUSTRIA

· Budapest

HUNGARY

ROMANIA

SLOVENIA

· Zagreb

CROATIA

· Copsa Mica

BOSNIA

Bucharest ·

YUGOSLAVIA

Belgrade

Danube R.

SERBIA

BULGARIA

ITALY

· Sofia

Black

ALBANIA

Sea

GREECE

0   500 KM.

TURKEY

500 MI.

R.P. Swanson

45

The priority given to Czech mothers for mineral water is one example that the lack of potable water has reached alarming proportions in that country. So, too, are frequent outbreaks of typhus, cholera and dysentery throughout the past decade.

In Poland, government figures indicate that approximately one-half of the country's water is unfit even for industrial use. Most of the Vistula River fits into that category, and the section that flows through Krakow is said to be "virtually devoid of biological life." Every single river in the Katowice region of southwest Poland is polluted "beyond all acceptable levels."

Much of this effluent flows into the Baltic Sea. The Vistula, which empties into the Bay of Gdansk, alone accounts for two-thirds of the 131,000 metric tons of nitrogen that end up in the Baltic each year. It also deposits 5,000 tons of phosphorus, and three tons each of highly toxic phenol and lead, as well as unspecified amounts of mercury, cadmium, zinc, and other heavy metals. As a result, vacationers at seaside resorts can no longer swim, children cannot even play in the wet sand due to dangerous bacteria counts, and much of the bay's fish contain excessive levels of mercury.

Air Unfit to Breathe

Eastern Europe's burning of abundant high-sulfur brown coal, combined with a lack of scrubbers and other pollution control equipment, has made the air quality in some regions among the worst in the world. Significantly, while emissions of major pollutants in the West have generally been steady or declining over the past decade because of regulatory actions and structural changes in economies, in Eastern Europe they continue to increase.

As in the West, the most pervasive air pollutants are sulfur dioxide, nitrogen oxides, suspended particulates and hydrocarbons. They are emitted primarily by power plants, factories and home furnaces.

The Eastern European nations are major emitters of sulfur dioxide—the pollutant for which data is most complete—with East Germany, Czechoslovakia and Poland among the world's top 12. Czechoslovakia, which uses brown coal for 60 percent of its production, has extraordinarily high rates of sulfur dioxide emissions, as well as of nitrogen oxides and hydrocarbons. When the even larger amount of sulfur dioxide that is blown in from neighboring states is added to the domestic total, Czechoslovakia holds the dubious distinction of having the highest density of sulfur dioxide deposits in Europe—an incredible 228 pounds per acre each year.

Because the bulk of the country's electricity generation takes place on the outskirts of the capital, wintertime sulfur dioxide concentrations in Prague average 20 times the legal maximum, according to a report by its city council. The capital is near the center of the region known as Bohemia, the northern part of which is so flooded with industrial by-products and pollutants blown across the border from East Germany that children are taken out of the area on weekends and kept inside their schools on especially unhealthy days.

Despite the fact that Poland is endowed with more low-sulfur coal than its neighbors, it still has the third highest per-acre deposit of sulfur dioxide in Europe. Part of the reason is that the government exports much of the low-sulfur coal to earn much-needed foreign exchange.

Air pollution in nearly every major city in Poland is reportedly 50 times above permissible limits, though the worst problems are concentrated in the southern industrial region of Silesia. The Krakow district and upper Silesia, which between them occupy less than three percent of Poland's territory, account for one-third of the particulate and half of the gaseous emissions.

"All around are signs of a city slowly rotting from pollution," writes Don Hinrichsen about Krakow in the *Amicus Journal.* "Pieces of masonry regularly fall off church steeples, balconies crumble and graceful, sculpted saints lack faces. What centuries of war and pestilence have spared, chemical pollutants have destroyed."

Dying Forests

Similarly, centuries-old forests are being decimated. Though the relationship between dying forests and air pollution and acid rain is the subject of some debate, the evidence that they are linked is strong.

Alarming portions of Eastern Europe's forested areas are afflicted with the *Waldsterben* – German for "forest death" – that has affected vast portions of Western Europe as well. United Nations data suggest that in four of the six Eastern European countries, a quarter to a third of the forests are damaged.

In Yugoslavia, the most recent estimates suggest that nearly half of the nation's coniferous forests are damaged. In both Poland and East Germany, private groups have estimated that the damage is far more extensive than the official figures indicate. And certain regions within countries are far more damaged than others; nearly all of the forests in the province of Katowice are damaged.

The devastation is most apparent along the border between Czechoslovakia and East Germany. "The Erzgebirge Mountains along the Czech-East German border are rapidly becoming the world's best showcase of the effects of acid rain," according to one observer. "At the top of some mountains, not a single tree survives – just barren landscape with a few remaining stumps."

The destruction of the forests is also an economic and ecological tragedy. Forest product industries, traditionally important to the region, will sustain enormous losses. Extensive deforestation will result in erosion and disruption of the water balance, as well as the destruction of many of the species supported by the woodlands.

The Danger to Health

Attempts to draw links between environmental decline and human health are a tricky business. Nevertheless, there are strong indications that in certain regions of Eastern Europe, air and water pollution are exacting a heavy toll.

One of the primary ways in which pollutants enter the body is through the food supply. A quarter of Poland's soil is believed to be too contaminated for safe farming. The government is considering a ban on growing vegetables in Silesia, where garden samples register concentrations of heavy metals – lead, zinc, cadmium and mercury – that are between 30 and 70 percent higher than World Health Organization norms. Measurements of lead and cadmium in the soil of the upper Silesian towns of Olkosz and Slawkow are the highest recorded anywhere in the world.

The widespread exposure to contaminated air, water and

food—as well as to occupational hazards—is making itself felt in morbidity statistics. In Silesia, rates of respiratory ailments and cancer are 30 to 50 percent above the national average for Poland, and life expectancy is at least two years shorter. In 1985, press reports noted an "appalling increase" in the number of retarded school-age children in the region. In Krakow, where the main source of pollution is the Lenin ironworks, infant mortality is more than three times the national average.

In Prague and Bratislava, as well, there are strong indications that pollution is causing increased rates of various health problems. A report by the Prague city council claims that the health of its residents is far worse than the national average, with unusually high rates of respiratory, digestive and allergic diseases. An unofficial report published in 1987 by doctors and scientists in Bratislava claimed that the incidence of cancer in the region had risen by 35 percent in five years and that infant mortality was 65 percent higher than in 1960.

Public Revolt

When lives and livelihoods are threatened so directly, people do not sit idly by. In Eastern Europe, opposition groups did risk political persecution to demand that something be done. The Czechoslovakian youth ecological group Brontosaurus is aptly named. "We better do something quick or we, too, will be extinct," warns Frantisek Ruba, its founder.

Environmentalism is not completely new to the region. In its officially sponsored form it dates to the early seventies, when

49

Eastern Bloc governments created environmental groups in the aftermath of events like the UN-sponsored Stockholm Conference on the Environment.

In Hungary, independent environmentalism first emerged from the scientific community in the late seventies and is now firmly established. In Poland, environmentalism emerged as a major force in the heyday of the Solidarity movement in the early eighties. It was not until the mid-eighties, however, with the rise of *glasnost* in the (former) Soviet Union, that an environmental movement across the whole of Eastern Europe emerged. As explained by Barbara Jancar, a political scientist with the State University of New York at Brockport, "...*glasnost* stripped away the ideological and political underpinnings for suppression of this movement."

But it was the explosion of the nuclear power plant at Chernobyl in the Soviet Union that, in Jancar's words, "was the physical catalyst for the virtual legitimization of the activities of unofficial environmental groups. Groups had been in existence before that time. . .but after Chernobyl, they proliferated."

This is particularly true in Poland, which received more of the power plant's radioactive fallout than any other country in Eastern Europe. There are reportedly now over 2,000 environmental organizations in the country, most of them established after Chernobyl.

The reforms now being considered across much of Eastern Europe under the umbrella of *perestroika* — Gorbachev's phrase for economic restructuring — offer some hope that efficiency will improve, although the magnitude of the task is daunting. And though the reforms offer long-term benefits, the immediate goal of increasing production may entail its own environmental costs.

The costs of cleaning up the damage already done will be high, but they pale in comparison to the costs that will be incurred if the governments fail to act. In Poland minimum losses due to pollution of the environment are estimated to equal 10 percent of the country's annual GNP. Although spending on environmental protection has increased, it remains a pittance compared with what is needed. Finding the capital will not be easy in a region of the world that is already heavily indebted to Western banks. Without action, however, the expenses will only mount.

6 EASTERN EUROPE: CAULDRON OF POISON

EAST GERMANY: THE SMOKE GETS IN YOUR EYES

Carol Byrne

Carol Byrne is a foreign correspondent for the Minneapolis-based Star Tribune. *In this article, Byrne describes the appalling conditions of a small East German industrial town. East and West Germany are now united since the fall of communism in the former Soviet Union and Eastern Europe.*

Points to Consider

1. Briefly describe the living conditions in Espenhain, Germany.

2. Why would anyone live there?

3. Who is responsible for these conditions?

4. What effect does coal usage have on human health?

Carol Byrne "Espenhain, East Germany: Town Is Sad Example of Pollution's Cost," Minneapolis **Star Tribune,** May 1, 1990. Reprinted with permission of the **Star Tribune.**

The smoke gets into your throat and makes it raw. It fills your mouth with a nauseating, acidic taste; water is undrinkable.

The statistics on pollution in East Germany are so appalling as to be almost unbelievable — one-third of the rivers and forests dead, air pollution in the cities up to 100 times the safe level, life spans shortened by years. Unbelievable.

Come to Espenhain

But come to Espenhain and believe. You can't help it. The map says Espenhain is a small town just south of Leipzig, but it looks like it has been transported to Dante's Inferno. It's noon, but the sky is so dark that the streetlights have come on in front of the red brick factory that stretches for blocks along the main street of town. The building is run-down, with broken windows and a yard littered with rubbish.

Chimneys sprout from the roof, a forest of them, tall and short, narrow and wide. From every chimney smoke pours out, sometimes in small wisps, sometimes in thick, rolling plumes. Next door is a power station with four great cooling towers, cauldrons that send steam boiling upward and an unnatural rain misting downward.

White smoke, gray smoke, black smoke, sulfurous orange and yellow smoke — it fills the sky over Espenhain with a permanent poisonous cloud. The smoke gets in your eyes and makes them water. Soon you have to take your contact lenses out; you can't get them clean. The smoke gets into your throat and makes it raw. It fills your mouth with a nauseating, acidic taste; water is undrinkable.

The Grand Canyon

Across the road from the factory, the ground suddenly opens into a great, gaping hole that stretches to the horizon. It looks like the Grand Canyon, with craters and ridges, but this isn't a natural phenomenon.

It's a coal mine gouged deep into the earth. Through the haze, dim figures are moving — bulldozers, derricks, cranes and trains, dwarfed to toy-size by the immense pit. The sound of the machinery echoes in the thick air — clanks and distant toots, like foghorns.

The mine is encircled by its creations — more factories with

Illustration by Ron Swanson.

more smoke pouring from their chimneys. There's a glint of light in the sky, but it's not the sun; it's gases being burned off. A little farther down the road lies another mine, this one already emptied of its coal and converted into a dump. Huge cranes have started to fill it up with garbage and industrial waste.

The houses of Espenhain come right up to the gates of the factory. Their walls are stained a murky brown; cracked plaster is falling away from the underlying brick. Bicyclists are out, church bells are ringing, people are working in their gardens. Flowers bloom in Espenhain, but sniff them and all you smell is sulfur.

This Is Our Home

Why would anyone live here? "You have to understand, for a long time we didn't realize what was happening to us," said Walter Christian Steinbach, leader of a local citizens' effort to do something about the pollution.

"When we started to suspect something was wrong, the government refused to talk to us so we knew nothing for sure. "Besides, this is our home. What would you have us do? There are 80,000 people in this district alone. We can't all move away." Ecological disaster came to Espenhain and its neighbors in the guise of progress.

Industrial Zone

After World War II, the Soviet Union created an Eastern

European industrial zone from southern Poland to northern Czechoslovakia. Its heart is in East Germany, which became one of the world's top 10 industrial nations, producing synthetic rubber, gas, chemicals, plastics, fertilizers, machinery, precision instruments, optical equipment and cameras.

Eastern Germany had always been an industrial area, but before the war it was powered by hard coal from the western part of the country. When that fuel was cut off after the war, East Germany turned to the only fuel it had in abundance — the soft, brown lignite coal mined around Espenhain.

It isn't just used for industry; people also heat their homes with it. Heaps of it lie everywhere — on sidewalks, in back yards. Its acrid tang is the smell of Eastern Europe. And that's the heart of the problem: lignite is full of sulfur. Every year millions of tons of sulfur dioxide are poured into the atmosphere from Eastern Europe. It returns as acid rain, it contributes to global warming, and its by-products cause cancer.

But it's not just the lignite fuel. Eastern factories have been dumping chemical wastes directly into the rivers, which are also afflicted with nitrates from fertilizer run-off. Drinking water is contaminated far above the minimum standards of the West.

The toll can be seen over and over in East Germany. The Elbe River is the most polluted in Europe. Bitterfeld (whose name aptly translates as "bitter field") sends school children to an island in the Baltic Sea for a month every year to escape the pollution, which is more than a pound per square yard per month. Wolfen, home of the nation's largest photochemical plant, is just as bad.

And Espenhain has the world's highest rate of sulfur dioxide pollution. "In this little district, we get 15 million tons a year," Steinbach said. "Last winter as an experiment I put a brass candlestick out on my balcony, just standing in the air. Before spring it was all corroded away."

Steinbach, 45, is a minister who lives in Roetha, the next town down the road from Espenhain. He has a raspy voice and bloodshot eyes, both of which he blames on the pollution. People were happy when the factories came, he said, because they provided jobs for virtually all of the district's 15,000 workers. But after a while, people in his congregation began to talk.

"It seemed that people were getting sick more, dying earlier," Steinbach said. "The doctor noticed symptoms of problems with people's lungs, but he was told to be quiet. We had nothing concrete, and it was forbidden to talk about these things. When I made inquiries of the government, I was threatened with arrest."

What Can Be Done?

Steinbach got together with 25 other local people to form a group called Ecolion (the lion is the symbol of the city of Leipzig) to pressure the government to protect the environment. It got little official response, but planted thousands of trees on its own.

The official silence ended when the Communist government was thrown out in 1989, and now Steinbach can quantify the area's problems: One of every two children has lung problems, one of every three children has heart problems, adults are biologically six years older than their chronological age, life expectancy is four years less than in the rest of the country.

What can be done for Espenhain? Steinbach says there is only one solution, and it's a drastic one: "We want to close everything down within a year. Close factories, close the mines. The nation will have to stop using lignite coal." Already Steinbach's group says it has collected 90,000 signatures supporting its position from throughout the country.

The implications of such a move are enormous: East Germany's industrial base would have to be rebuilt. Hard coal would have to be imported, driving up consumer, heating and electrical costs. Espenhain's workers would have to be retrained, and new industries would have to be developed.

Western experts have estimated that it would take 20 years and $200 billion to clean up the mess, if a cleanup is even possible. Does Steinbach really think such a huge change could be made? "Let's face it. Without help from the outside world, it won't happen."

EASTERN EUROPE:
CAULDRON OF POISON

POLAND: IS IT LOST?

Sabine Rosenbladt

Sabine Rosenbladt is a German writer specializing in Eastern European environmental issues. Environmental conditions in Poland have changed little since she wrote this article when the communist government was still in power.

Points to Consider:

1. How bad is the water quality of the Vistula River?

2. What has happened to Poland's fishing industry?

3. What is the status of drinking water in Poland?

4. When are improvements expected in Poland's air quality?

Excerpted from an article by Sabine Rosenbladt titled, "Is Poland Lost?" **Greenpeace Magazine,** November/December 1988.

By the year 2000, say some observers, not a drop of Poland's water will be clean enough to be used for anything.

The river around which the port city of Gdansk grew is called the Vistula. On its way through the heart of Poland, it passes through many large and small cities, most of which dump their raw sewage directly into it. Half of the 813 Polish communities that line the banks of the Vistula, including the capitol city of Warsaw, have no sewage treatment facilities. Some 10,000 industrial polluters also do without waste treatment.

As a result, the Vistula is so polluted that along 81 percent of the river's length, the water is too dirty even for industrial use; it would corrode heavy machinery. The river flushes some 90,000 tons of nitrogen and 5,000 tons of phosphorus into the Baltic, along with 80 tons of mercury, cadmium, zinc, lead, copper, phenol, and chlorinated hydrocarbons.

The filth collects in the bay, where it is further enriched by the sewage from Gdansk, Gdynia and Sopot. Polish newspapers report that the waters of the Baltic near Gdansk "exceed bacterial standards for waste water by at least one hundred times, due to sewage dumping". In 1981, the Polish newspaper *Szpilki* caricatured the Baltic as a gigantic toilet bowl.

This story is being repeated throughout Poland. In 1985, the Sejm, (Polish parliament) recognized four areas of the country, including Gdansk Bay, as "ecological disaster areas." The industrial district of Upper Silesia, the Krakow area and the copper basin of Liegnitz/Glogow shared the distinction. "Disaster area" is meant literally. By Poland's own environmental standards, the regions are so contaminated with industrial and municipal pollution that the people living there should be evacuated. This is not an option, however, for these places are home to 11 million people, or 30 percent of Poland's population.

Gdansk's long sandy beaches have been closed for years. The seven nations that border the landlocked Baltic Sea have been poisoning it each year with about 15,000 tons of heavy metals, a million tons of nitrogen, 70,000 tons of phosphorous, 50,000 tons of oil and highly toxic PCBs. While the Helsinki Convention of 1974 contains a pledge by these countries to limit damages "as much as possible", the promise remains unfulfilled. In 1988, 100,000 square kilometers of the sea floor were found to be biologically dead. Extinction threatens seals, starfish, mussels, crabs, and gray seals. Algal blooms and dead fish float on the brackish waters.

A day's fishing in Gdansk Bay often yields little more than a few hundred pounds of diseased flounder. ©Karl Markusen, **Greenpeace,** Germany.

Foul Water

"This looks awful," says fisherman Pawel Krampikowski as he examines the sample that Greenpeace diver Dave Greenway brought up from the sea floor at a depth of four meters. Jet black, oily debris floats in the jar. "No wonder there aren't any fish anymore," says the ethnic German, a descendent of generations of Baltic fishermen. "You can't imagine the fish that used to live in this bay—perch, pike, roach, and eel—tons and tons of them. And herring, flounder, cod. Now there is nothing left. Nothing."

The official catch statistics support his assessment. Though Poland has an annual fishing quota of 200,000 tons, in 1984 Polish fishermen caught only 50,000 tons. In 1986, the catch declined to less than 28,000 tons. The last eels that were caught here were corroded by toxic chemicals, says Karola Palka, a resident of Sopot. "They looked like they were already cooked."

A few hundred pounds of sick flounder per night is all that the residents of Sopot, with their small boats and nets, can get out of the Baltic. Now they fear that even this will soon be forbidden. How contaminated are the fish? Palka displays her bare feet: mosquito bites have swelled into purulent sores after contact with the Baltic seawater.

Wearing a dry suit, Greenpeace campaigner Rune Eriksen dives into the mouth of the Vistula River. After only half a meter, he can no longer see his hand in front of his face. The water is black. A dirty broth gushes everywhere from effluent pipes leading from Gdansk's industrial installations — petroleum refineries, phosphate processors and a sulfur plant at which pure sulfur is stored outside in a huge bright yellow pile that leaches into the water table. Waste water treatment costs 6-12 zloty per cubic meter. In contrast, companies pay only 1.2 zloty in fines for every cubic meter of raw waste dumped. The government even subsidizes its industries for the fines they must pay. Dumping is a lot cheaper.

They still call what comes out of most Polish taps "drinking water", but only for reasons of nostalgia. According to 1984 official Polish environmental statistics, "71 percent of drinking water samples were disqualified by the national public health authorities for reasons of hygiene." By the year 2000, say some observers, not a drop of Poland's water will be clean enough to be used for anything.

Environmental Movement

Of the literally hundreds of small regional groups in Poland, Polski Klub Ekologiczny (PKE), the Polish Ecological Club, is the acknowledged leader. Founded in 1980 in Krakow, it today has 15 regional offices and 6,000 members across the country.

In 1981, the PKE and allies in the trade union succeeded in closing down the Skawina Aluminum Works, a plant nine miles south of Krakow whose fluorine emissions had so damaged the environment that cows in the neighboring fields were no longer able to walk. In Upper Silesia, the club sees to it that local school children escape the extremely damaging, poisoned air at least once a year and get out into the country.

In Warsaw, club members have been locked in a hot battle with the local bureaucracy and construction industry over the fate of the last urban green spaces. In Miedzyrzecz, near Poznan, the club organized opposition to a planned nuclear waste site so effectively that the plans were shelved. And in Gdansk, the PKE is currently trying to prevent Poland's first nuclear power plant from being built.

Chernobyl turned Polish environmentalists from moderate supporters of nuclear power (coal is the principal source of

---

SECRET RECORDS IN BULGARIA

In Bulgaria, the leaders decided decades ago to chronicle secretly the health effects of their industrial revolution.

Disease was rampant in people living near heavy industrial complexes. In one of the most extreme cases, some people near a lead and zinc smelting plant in Kurjali, in southern Bulgaria, had 333 micrograms of lead for each hundred milliliters of blood. The international standard is 30 to 50 micrograms.

Josh Friedman, "The Hidden Cost of Industrialization in Bulgaria," **Newsday,** April 24, 1990.

Poland's air pollution) into determined antinuclear activists. AKW Zarnowiec, (a nuclear power plant) which is currently being built near Gdansk and is scheduled to go into operation in 1992, has already been dubbed "Zernobyl" by locals.

"This thing is supposed to cost $5 billion, which is equivalent to the annual income of 15 billion Poles over three years," groans biophysicist Jerzy Jaskowski. "It's amazing! We need that money urgently in order to cope with the ecological disasters.

Air Pollution in Krakow

At first glance, the well-groomed front yards on Zaleskiego Street in Krakow look perfectly normal. A closer look reveals lilacs, privet hedges, hydrangea, apple blossoms and rosebushes, all strangely mutated. In many places, they have sprouted curious, bonsai-like stunted leaves. Trees are completely barren; even the weeds at the edge of the street show signs of failing.

"Chlorinated hydrocarbons, chloroform, trichloroethylene, acetone, methanol," says Maria Guminska, founding member of PKE, pointing to a dilapidated factory building at the end of the street. "It all came from there." POLFA, the pharmaceutical company that occupies the site, "supposedly manufactures vitamin C. It isn't possible to get any more details." In response to their neighbors' protests, plant managers installed filters. "But now they emit poisons at night. You can smell it, that sweet smell. We are completely defenseless against it. The authorities refused to take any action."

Chlorinated hydrocarbons belong to the most dangerous of all toxins. They build up in the brain, liver, kidneys, heart and reproductive organs, attack the central nervous system, and cause cancer. Maria Guminska: "In my building alone, 23 residents have died in the last ten years of cancer, including my husband. My child was born completely deformed, but they tell me that these number are not statistically significant."

The west wind blows in tons of toxic dust laden with heavy metals, sulfur, and nitrous oxide from Upper Silesia; when the east wind blows, the filth comes in even greater concentrations from Nowa Huta, the enormous steel complex in the eastern part of the city.

Krakow is enveloped in a stationary cloud of smog 135 days of the year. This causes the facades of the buildings in the medieval city center to crumble even faster; the corroding vapors have even decomposed the gold roof of the Sigismund Chapel. And in the old part of town, the oxygen content can drop from a normal of 21 percent to 17 percent, making the atmosphere literally fatal for heart patients, asthmatics and old people.

The lifespan of Krakow residents is three to four years shorter than that of their fellow countrymen. The chances of developing lung cancer are twice as high here. PKE doctors have determined that the residents of this city suffer in disproportionately high numbers from allergies, chronic bronchitis, degenerative bone diseases, arteriosclerosis and circulatory illnesses. And the infant mortality rate, at over 2.5 per thousand inhabitants, is more than one-and-one-half times the national average.

No Improvement in Sight

Conditions in Krakow are surpassed by those of Upper Silesia. This coal-producing and heavily industrialized region holds the uncontested world record for all kinds of pollution. Upper Silesia produces 60 percent of Poland's industrial waste, 40 percent of its gas emissions and 30 percent of the toxic particulates. According to official statistics, in two-thirds of the region, all the emissions standards for particulates, gases and heavy metals are continually broken by wide margins.

There is no improvement in sight. Until the year 2000, emissions will continue to rise, according to pessimistic assessments by the PKE. The sulfur dioxide content alone is expected to go from the current total of approximately 5 million tons annually to 9.1 million tons. Today, 60 percent of Polish forests are sick and hundreds of thousands of hectares of ground are devastated.

A 1983 report from the government and the World Health Organization about the Glogow region predicts "emissions from the copper industry will double by 1990. It is therefore likely that public health standards will be seriously and frequently broken and that the health of the surrounding population will worsen."

Yet everywhere in the disaster area, contaminated fields continue to be farmed. The result: 20 percent of the food products tested were classified as hazardous to public health by the authorities. Among other things, vegetables were found to contain 220 times the limit for cadmium, 165 for zinc, 134 for lead, 34 for fluorine, and 2.5 times for uranium. Green lettuce, grown in the vicinity of the Boleslaw zinc plant near Krakow, contained 230 milligrams of lead per kilo. A kilo of cabbage held 30 milligrams of lead, a kilo of onions, 42.

Lead causes brain damage, particularly in children. The 1983 report noted an "alarming increase" in the number of retarded children in Upper Silesia.

Desperate Condition

Poland is in desperate condition. Waldemar Michna, Poland's Environment Minister, assessed the total environmental damage in his country at one billion zlotys annually. "That is between 10 and 15 percent of the Polish national income." The country as a whole, according to Polish estimates, needs at least 6,000 treatment plants. It also needs to drastically reshape and upgrade the machinery that makes up its industrial base, for economic as well as environmental reasons.

"Ecological economics must be the goal," agrees Michna. "And on large projects, such as saving the Baltic, there can't be any prejudices. We must all work together." Bronislaw Kaminski, environmental director in the dying city of Krakow, even has a crazy dream: in twenty years he wants to turn Krakow into a European model city for environmental protection. "Krakow is indeed the acid test," he says, without smiling. "If we can get Krakow back on its feet, then we'll manage the rest, too."

ROMANIA: MEDICAL NEEDS ARE OVERWHELMING

Carol Byrne

Carol Byrne is a foreign correspondent for the Minneapolis-based Star Tribune. *In this article Byrne describes government inaction, and the desperate need for medical facilities in Romania.*

Points to Consider:

1. Who is responsible for the conditions in Copsa Mica, Romania?

2. What is the "invisible fallout" from the local factories?

3. Describe the symptoms of air pollution in Copsa Mica.

4. How have the health threats affected life expectancy?

Carol Byrne "Air Pollution Darkens Lives in Romanian Town," **Star Tribune,** June 22, 1990. Reprinted with permission of the **Star Tribune.**

"Out of 3,860 employees, 3,500 are on the list of being poisoned with lead, with varying degrees of severity. In 30 years of industrial medicine, I've never seen anything like this. This place is an Auschwitz."

Sinna lives near the edge of Copsa Mica, a town of 6,000 in north-central Romania. Its postcard-perfect setting, a river valley amid forested mountains, is spoiled by two poisonous factories that have turned it into one of the most polluted places on Earth. Together, the factories contaminate the air and the inhabitants with 30,000 tons of particles a year.

The endless soot comes from the carbosin factory, which annually produces 3,000 tons of a fine, black powder used to make tires, typographical inks and pharmaceuticals.

But it's not this very visible pollution that is so dangerous; it's the invisible fallout from the IMMN metal factory next door. IMMN annually produces 56,000 tons of zinc derivatives that are used in everything from animal feed to aeronautics to lamp filaments. In the process, it poisons its workers with lead and fills the air for miles around with sulfur dioxide.

The combination has blighted vegetation, made the ground crunch underfoot, streaked the ducks, the chickens and the children black. Bad as Copsa Mica looks today, it's better than it was in the days of dictator Nicolae Ceausescu. Half of its production lines are closed down now as Romania's new government starts to try to clean up the mess.

Medical Needs

Dr. Jean Nenea is middle-aged, over-worked and grumpy. He rushes about his office in the metal factory's clinic, treating an endless stream of patients and practically shouting out his frustrations. "Out of 3,860 employees, 3,500 are on the list of being poisoned with lead, with varying degrees of severity," he said. "In 30 years of industrial medicine, I've never seen anything like this. This place is an Auschwitz."

"We need money, we need nurses, we can't cope anymore. Out of six doctors, I'm the only one left here." On the average, he said, he sends two patients a day away to hospitals and sanitariums to be treated for lead poisoning. The symptoms: anemia, extreme nervousness, severe stomach pains, nerve paralysis, vomiting, constipation, occasionally encephalitis.

And it's not just the workers, he said. "I can tell the whole population has been affected by lead. The children are caught

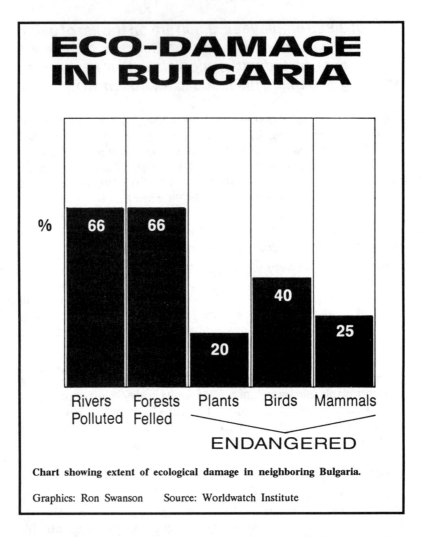

ECO-DAMAGE IN BULGARIA

%	66	66	

Rivers Polluted | Forests Felled | Plants 20 | Birds 40 | Mammals 25

ENDANGERED

Chart showing extent of ecological damage in neighboring Bulgaria.

Graphics: Ron Swanson   Source: Worldwatch Institute

by absorbing it from the air, the animals don't live long, the grass is full of soot. And besides lead, there is general poisoning from the sulfur dioxide." Local hospitals report an increase in congenital heart defects in newborn children, and the infant mortality rate is very high at an estimated 30 per 1,000.

The list of problems spirals on and on: alcoholism and malnutrition, causing impotence, causing the breakup of families, causing heart attacks from hypertension in men as young as 25. All in all, the life span in Copsa Mica is about five years shorter than elsewhere in Romania.

The physical problems lead to lots of industrial accidents at the plant—on this particular day, Nenea already has treated five accident victims and it's only early afternoon.

At the clinic for the soot plant, Dr. Alexandru Balog is more resigned and philosophical. "When I got here eight years ago, it took me only two minutes to realize something was wrong," he said. "But the answer was always, 'Production must go on,' and 'Make change if you want, but don't spend any money.' I don't even have a nurse, but I've stopped talking about it. What's the use?"

Balog said that the main problems from the soot are skin irritations. Sulfur dioxide fallout also causes breathing problems ranging from bronchitis to asthma to pneumonia. Industrial wastes are dumped into the river, which is now dead below the plant. "I don't drink the water in this town," Balog said.

He said it will take more than anti-pollution devices to clean up Copsa Mica. "We also need a change in attitude because during the old regime we got so isolated from the modern world. All 23 million of us Romanians should be transported outside our boundaries to see Europe and the rest of the world, so we know what is possible."

Copsa Mica has taken a step in that direction. About 150 local children have been sent to Austria for a six-week "refresher", thanks to a Belgian relief group.

Government Inaction

The factory complex sprawls along the riverbank, a blackened jumble of smokestacks, cooling towers, metal walkways, tanks, cranes and wires. With its broken windows and its rusted and corroded metals, it looks like it might come tumbling down at any moment.

Black figures are moving about—workers with their clothes, hands and faces grimed black so that only their eyes shine out. One carries a loaf of bread, also coated with soot. The workers are happy that the new government has increased their pay, given them a bonus for dangerous work, raised their retirement benefits and boosted their vacations from 15 days a year to 24. But they still say their lives are hard.

Nicolae Nicula: "The health problems are misery, but you get used to the atmosphere. Many people who work here don't understand what it's all about and don't know the danger. They just put in their time and get their money."

Nicolae Cioraru: "I've been here 24 years and always felt all right. I don't go to the medical checkups because I don't want

67

to know." Cornel Fageteanu: "I lost the sight in my right eye when a metal fragment flew into it—we don't have goggles. So we must live our lives like this and be satisfied. What do we know? We go from home to work and back again and that's all. I am just glad I am still alive."

Both of the factories were built with help from abroad, the soot plant in 1952 and the metals plant in the mid-1960s. Then in the mid-70s, Ceausescu ordered them to cut off all contact with the outside world. Since then, upgrading or modernization has been extremely difficult. The workers have had to improvise their own repairs, make their own new parts, devise their own technologies.

"It's a tribute to our engineers that we were able to keep functioning at all," said commercial director Ovidiu Ilies. "In addition, the old government did not allow us to stop production in order to do any modernization work as we wanted. Instead, they kept raising our quotas. We couldn't stop."

Ilies said the factory staff told the Ceausescu government time and again that the plant had pollution problems, but always got the same answer. "The situation has been taken into account and we'll do everything possible."

"But nothing ever changed," Ilies said.

"The government didn't want to hear that we had problems," said Radu Ciorbanu, an official at the soot plant. "The fact that they asked us to produce so much meant that they didn't take our complaints seriously. Last year, we achieved only 80 percent of our production quota, meaning our wages were docked accordingly."

Both men said that their workers need protective equipment, such as overalls, gloves, goggles and steel-tipped shoes. "Such equipment doesn't exist anywhere in this country," Ilies said.

Their hope is now that the new revolutionary government has allowed them to restore foreign contacts, they will find help from abroad. In the meantime, the government has permitted them to cut production to get started on modernization and anti-pollution work.

The metal plant has shut down its second line of production, and the soot plant has closed four of its seven ovens. But Ciorbanu said that the best the soot plant could hope for would be to reduce its pollution by 20 percent. "For the time being, we do not have conditions to reconstruct everything, as we should do and as we would like to do," he said.

"In an ideal world, we would tear all this down and start over."

WHAT IS POLITICAL BIAS?

This activity may be used as an individualized study guide for students in libraries and resource centers or as a discussion catalyst in small group and classroom discussions.

Many readers are unaware that written material usually expresses an opinion or bias. The skill to read with insight and understanding requires the ability to detect different kinds of bias. Political bias, race bias, sex bias, ethnocentric bias and religious bias are five basic kinds of opinions expressed in editorials and literature that attempt to persuade. This activity will focus on political bias defined in the glossary below.

Five Kinds of Editorial Opinion or Bias

Sex Bias — the expression of dislike for and/or feeling of superiority over a person because of gender or sexual preference

Race Bias — the expression of dislike for and/or feeling of superiority over a racial group

Ethnocentric Bias — the expression of a belief that one's own group, race, religion, culture or nation is superior. Ethnocentric persons judge others by their own standards and values.

Political Bias — the expression of opinions and attitudes about government-related issues on the local, state, national or international level

Religious Bias — the expression of a religious belief or attitude

---

Guidelines

Read through the following statements and decide which ones represent *political opinion* or *bias*. Evaluate each statement by using the method indicated below.

- Mark (P) — for statements that reflect political opinion or bias.

- Mark (F) — for any factual statements.

- Mark (O) — for statements of opinion that reflect

70

other kinds of opinion or bias.

- **Mark (N) — for any statements that you are not sure about.**

___ 1. The statistics on pollution in East Germany are so appalling as to be unbelievable.

___ 2. It will take 20 years and $200 billion to clean up the mess.

___ 3. Forty years of socialism has left Eastern Europe in ecological turmoil.

___ 4. The re-unification of Germany was a necessary first step to correct the environmental destruction in the east.

___ 5. Bulgaria's government-owned factories are guilty of dumping toxins and waste into the rivers at night.

___ 6. To modernize Bulgaria's polluting industries will take a huge investment from western governments.

___ 7. Unreasonable quotas are to blame for high levels of pollution in Romania's factory towns.

___ 8. Air pollution in Romania has caused an increase in a wide variety of health problems.

___ 9. Nuclear energy is a partial solution to air pollution in Czechoslovakia.

___10. Market-based prices should be applied to energy used by public and industrial consumers in Czechoslovakia.

___11. One of the roadblocks to cleaning up Eastern Europe is the huge debt carried by most governments.

___12. Eastern Europe must reduce its reliance on energy sources from the Russian Republic.

Other Activities

1. Locate three examples of *political opinion* or *bias* in the readings from Chapter Two.

2. Make up one sentence statements that would be an example of each of the following: *sex bias, race bias, ethnocentric bias,* and *religious bias.*

CHAPTER 3

REVERSING THE TREND: IDEAS IN CONFLICT

9

REVERSING THE TREND:
IDEAS IN CONFLICT

A MARKET APPROACH WILL
HELP THE ENVIRONMENT

James M. Sheehan

James M. Sheehan is a research associate at the Competitive Enterprise Institute in Washington, D.C.

Points to Consider:

1. How will overt Western aid hinder the clean-up of Eastern Europe?

2. Why is central planning bad for the environment?

3. Why is a free market approach the answer?

4. How are individual property rights important? Explain.

James M. Sheehan, "The Greening of Eastern Europe", **Global Affairs,** Spring, 1992.

Rather than allowing bureaucrats to control the environmental and economic agendas, the emerging governments of Eastern Europe should pursue—and should be encouraged to pursue—a free market agenda.

The unvarnished truth about Eastern Europe's disastrous condition—both economically and ecologically—is fast becoming conventional wisdom. What once was the breadbasket of Europe is now its basket case. The degradation of the Eastern European environment is arguably the most advanced of anywhere on the globe; indeed, the revolutions against totalitarianism included "green" organizations dismayed over the potential health effects of a deteriorating environment. Setting an increasingly hyperbolic tone, the national assembly of the Yugoslav republic of Montenegro proclaimed itself the world's first "ecological state" in September 1991. A group of citizens in Bulgaria threatened not so long ago to seek "ecological asylum" in other countries.

As the new governments of Eastern Europe stabilize politically, they will have to clean up the contaminants inherited from former communist regimes and modernize the incredibly inefficient and polluting industrial infrastructure. Initial estimates of the costs of environmental cleanup for the region range into the hundreds of billions of dollars. Cleanup of the Danube River alone may cost $10 billion, according to World Bank environmental specialist Stephen Lintner. These enormous sums have led many in the West to argue the necessity of massive infusions of state-to-state aid. But a number of misconceptions about the fragile process of transition threaten to cause such foreign aid to be misappropriated for a kind of Potemkin environmentalism: all facade, and no solid foundations.

Myths about Foreign Aid

Foreign aid officials in the West are currently providing extensive guidance to the newly democratizing Eastern European governments in an effort to insure that their emerging market-oriented economies will contain sufficient safeguards for the ecology. Foreign aid programs administered by U.S. officials include numerous provisions designed to encourage the enactment of strict environmental standards and regulations. America's answer to the environmental damage of socialism, surprisingly, is a re-institutionalization of bureaucratic state control.

75

Yet if four decades of Eastern European history demonstrate anything, it is that nothing can be worse for the environment than central planning. The prevailing theme of the recent revolutions against communism holds that free markets based in sound property rights offer the best prospects for both the economy and the environment. However, these economic and environmental values in Eastern Europe are threatened by a veritable honor roll of myths inspiring American efforts to support the transition to market economies—half-truths invoked in order to justify continued and massive government interference.

Myth 1: Western assistance for the environmental cleanup of Eastern Europe will create an enormous new market that will reignite the regional economy.

Fact: The environmental cleanup of Eastern Europe will have little positive impact on the economies of that region insofar as the cleanup is directed by government authorities. The money spent on the cleanup will be redistributed wealth—whether provided externally or from within. No wealth is created by this vast "new" market.

Myth 2: The enactment of stringent environmental laws is necessary to develop the overall perception of "social progress" in Eastern Europe's transformation.

Fact: Depressed economies are the predictable result of slow growth policies, and they will more likely perpetuate a perception of stagnation and decline. If Western firms are to clean up Eastern European contaminants, a dependence on the West will result.

Stringent environmental regulations would also choke off foreign investment that is not subsidized. Sound, calculated investments, made for their potential to realize profits, are the only type that can sustain wealth and job creation in the long term.

Myth 3: Eastern European governments must coordinate national industrial policies and control foreign investment to ensure that environmental concerns are taken into account.

Fact: In the previous communist regimes, trade protectionism was a chief culprit in environmental destruction. In keeping out western industry, indigenous technology was protected from competition. Antiquated, environment-polluting technology was thus preserved in its most destructive form, with no incentive for innovation.

Myth 4: A global environmental strategy would first direct funds to regions in greatest crisis, namely Eastern Europe.

Fact: This is analogous to saying that all social programs would be more effective if funds were transferred to only the poorest of the poor. It ignores the role of incentives in cleaning up the environment. If individuals are allowed to own resources, these assets will directly benefit from wise management practices.

If Eastern Europe's ecology has indeed reached crisis proportions, then a system based on a broad distribution of property rights would be much more effective than "emergency" cash infusions to government bureaucracies.

Myth 5: Institutional strengthening of government agencies and environmental organizations will protect the environment by fostering public awareness and concern about pollution.

Fact: This strategy simply feeds the interest group frenzy that hinders true environmental progress.

It must be recognized that Eastern European governments are still dominated by opportunistic lifetime bureaucrats. Before providing them with money and expertise to continue their domination of their nations' economic systems, Western assistance should as a matter of absolute priority promote development of the private sector. A free-market strategy would provide built-in incentives for pollution prevention, spread out over the entire economy, not just calibrated to narrow interests.

Myth 6: A Western-style government regulatory bureaucracy must be used to protect the environment from unrestrained capitalism.

Fact: Centrally-planned economies in Eastern Europe had very strict environmental laws — on paper. These laws were unenforceable because they distorted the prices of natural resources; therefore, such resources were not distributed according to their true value to society. Capitalism, unrestrained or otherwise, has done a superior job of protecting the environment — always has, always will.

The Free Market Solution

Rather than allowing bureaucrats to control the environmental and economic agendas, the emerging governments of Eastern Europe should pursue — and should be encouraged to pursue — a free market agenda:

- The establishment of constitutionally-enforceable property rights and private contract rights;

- accurate, market-based pricing of natural resources, free from government distortions;
- An infrastructure to handle mediation of private contractual disputes; and
- privatization, or "Ecological Homesteading", of collectively-owned resources.

An American Example

When European settlers in America first crossed the Appalachian Mountains, the land they found was owned by the national government, a situation not unlike that which exists in Eastern Europe today. By distributing ownership to individuals, the Homestead Act allowed the American midwest and western plains to become the preeminent agricultural region in the world. It allowed "homesteaders" to own land, provided they lived on it for at least five years. The success of the Homestead Act was unprecedented in human history. The failure of socialism in Eastern Europe is comparably unprecedented.

World War II, with its urgent demand for industrial production at any cost, led directly to the pollution of American air and water. The stagnant rivers and sooty skies of the 1950s and 1960s were not the result of unrestrained capitalism. They were the legacy of state-directed wartime production. In Eastern Europe, state-directed industrialization had a predictably similar effect—although the greater proportion of state control produced even worse environmental mishaps.

The lesson of the American experience is this: the people themselves must be empowered to protect their environmental and economic interests. After decades of centrally-directed abuses, the forests, the rivers, and the air of Eastern Europe are in critical disrepair. But more central planning will simply produce political trade-offs. Unlike America, which developed a strong economy through free enterprise and then imposed an environmental regulatory system, Eastern Europe has the unique opportunity to develop economic property rights that incorporate ecological values simultaneously.

Individual Rights

The dual crisis of the economy and the ecology is the direct result of socialism's denial of individual rights. The solution is to create and defend private rights throughout society—as a defense against political and bureaucratic tyranny. Likewise, private ecological rights offer the opportunity for Eastern Europeans to fight off a different, but related, encroachment of individual rights by excessive government control.

Political pressures from the West may require that individual property rights in Eastern European environmental amenities be given a more appealing name, such as "National Ecological Leases". They might even be perpetually renewable and freely transferable. In addition, particular aspects that comprise the whole must be severable. For instance, the homesteader must be able to assign or lease to others the rights to farm, hunt, plant trees, or fish on particular tracts of his land. Regional and municipal airsheds could be privatized, or at the very least placed under the control of local officials, directly responsible to the local population.

Ecological homesteading need not be limited to fishing ponds and potato farms. Forests should be distributed among those willing to live there and graze cattle, or manage for firewood, timber, and the like. Society would not necessarily be altered in radical ways under this proposal since the primary candidates for homesteading would be those who currently live or work on state farms. Ongoing privatization reforms may, under certain circumstances, grant priority to those who have legitimate claims against the former communist governments for previous confiscation of property.

It is well documented in the Soviet Union, for example, that private plots grow significantly more food than collectivized farmlands. Private ownership provides individuals with the incentive to make investments, which in turn reduce wastefulness. This example of stewardship of a scarce resource by self-interested "owners" should ease concern over widespread abuse of the environment if property rights are adopted in former socialist nations. Individuals always desire to capture the economic value of resources, and environmental resources are no different. Eastern European governments can harness that energy by encouraging markets to develop, rather than by continuing to drive them underground into an illegal "black" economy.

In the area of Western assistance, more attention must be given to private sector development as opposed to government-to-government loans. Private commercial banks are in a superior position to ascertain the needs of individuals for such things as homes, farm equipment, and training. Government-backed loans remove accountability from both the bureaucratic institutions involved and the recipients. The problem results from the phenomenon of an international lending wealthy elite taking money from taxpayers and transferring it to other unaccountable bureaucracies. Before the market economy is even developed, bureaucrats are attempting to develop an infrastructure by which they can regulate it.

Not a Champion

Despite its blemished record in promoting economic development, the U.S. foreign aid establishment now insists that it can be the champion of the global environment. Yet, with its long history of failure in managing traditional development, why should anyone expect it to be successful in managing ecologically sustainable development? Inept lending practices promise to beget an ecological version of the U. S. savings and loan crisis.

A comprehensive proposal for the reform of Western lending practices is beyond the scope of this paper. But, it should be noted that this aspect of U.S. foreign aid has its own implications for Eastern Europe's ecology, and could imperil its environmental well-being. The debt burdens being imposed on the undeveloped economic systems of the region will siphon off much of the new wealth that is generated — if, indeed, any is generated at all. Massive debt obligations will necessarily compete for economic resources with the productive and innovative sectors of the economy. Of vital importance to the environment is how quickly Eastern Europe can adopt environmentally-beneficial management techniques, customs, and institutions. Only a healthy private economy can achieve such goals.

10   REVERSING THE TREND: IDEAS IN CONFLICT

GREED IS NOT THE ANSWER

James Ridgeway

James Ridgeway is a columnist for the Village Voice. *This reading appeared as an article by Ridgeway in the* Multinational Monitor.

Points to Consider:

1. Who are the biggest polluters in the former Soviet Union?

2. How is foreign investment affecting the environment?

3. What steps are being taken to punish polluters?

4. What is the Socio-Ecological Union?

James Ridgeway, "Environmental Devastation in the (Former) Soviet Union," **Multinational Monitor,** September 1990.

Some people claim, and not without grounds, that many firms would like to develop their 'dirty' industries in our territory, such as ammoniac or pesticide productions.

A survey of the (former) Soviet Union's environmental situation reveals a country in desperate straits. According to a mapping scheme developed by Soviet scientists, 16 percent of their country, containing a quarter of its population, is at environmental risk. Various data paint a somber picture: 40 percent of the Soviet people live in areas where air pollutants are three to four times the maximum allowable levels. Sanitation is primitive. Where it exists, for example, in Moscow, it doesn't work properly. Half of all industrial waste water in the capital city goes untreated. In Leningrad, nearly half of the children have intestinal disorders caused by drinking contaminated water from what was once Europe's most pristine supply. Beaches along the Black, Azoz and Baltic Seas are frequently closed because of pollution, and numerous rivers in the European part of the (former) Soviet Union are off bounds because they are so filthy.

Taming the Polluting State

Nikolai Vorontsov, chairman of *Goskompriroda,* the state committee for the protection of nature (in the former Soviet Union), described the uphill fight to get any sort of a grip on environmental pollution. *Goskompriroda,* which was only started in 1988, employed just 450 people, compared with 600 in West Germany. The committee had only two computers, and a budget of 20 million rubles (less than $4 million) compared to the U.S. Environmental Protection Agency's budget of $5 billion. For the whole of the Soviet Union, which comprises one-sixth of the land mass of the planet, expenditures for environmental protection, besides those of Goskompriroda, amounted to a mere 10 million rubles.

The amount of resources allocated to environmental causes may seem ludicrous, but money was not the primary issue. The big question in Moscow was whether the state would police itself. On the surface, the stated intent and the laws were not bad. The government endorsed legislation to rehabilitate the Aral Sea and halted construction of nine half-built nuclear power plants. Beginning in 1991, polluting factories were to be fined, with 85 percent of the money going to local governmental institutions for pollution control.

Illustration by Ron Swanson

But the government's management of the Chernobyl disaster did not bode well for its self-regulating capabilities. After Chernobyl, livestock thought to be contaminated from the accident were killed so their meat would not be eaten. But some of the meat was transported to distant parts of the country, mixed with other meat and made into sausage. This was possible because the Ministry of Public Health had secretly made temporary rules raising the limits for radiation concentrations in meat.

Taming Foreign Polluters

Foreign investment, centered around extractive industries and tourism projects, poses another dilemma. The most advanced projects are schemes involving multinational corporations, including prominent U.S. firms which have stood by the Soviets through thick and thin: Armand Hammer's Occidental Petroleum and Cyrus Eaton's Cleveland firm.

In western Siberia, Japanese, West German, U.S. and Italian firms have begun work on five large petro-chemical projects in the Tyumen area, which environmentalists insist is on its way to becoming one of the world's great waste dumps. The nearby Ob River has been reduced to an oily sluice. Pipeline accidents number 600 per year. Just about everyone in the Soviet Union hates the project, except, of course, the Stalin-era ministries that are pushing it ahead. In March 1988, the Soviet Union made a deal with Occidental, the Japanese firm Marubeni and two Italian outfits — Montedison and ENI — to build a gas and chemical plant near Guriev in the Caspian. The total cost is $6 billion, and when it is finished the complex will be located near a gas-condensate plant at Astrakhan. The Astrakhan plant was equipped with a French-made pollution control system, which did not work, necessitating the evacuation of nearby villages. Scientists predict the same thing will happen with the new projects, which have the potential to produce an accident comparable in scale to Chernobyl.

Occidental is involved in two other environmentally destructive projects. One is the Ventspils Petrochemical Complex in Latvia, which processes petroleum products for export. Enormous amounts of toxic and flammable chemicals from the complex swirl through the city and around the countryside. Occidental signed another deal to expand a chemical plant that produces plastics in the Ukraine. It already is a major polluter, and each expansion is likely to make matters even worse. In both Latvia and the Ukraine, independent or local reform groups have mounted serious, ongoing opposition to these foreign projects.

The (former) Soviet populace is becoming wary of the likely environmental impacts of the multinational petrochemical corporations eager to invest in the USSR. "When *perestroika* began in the USSR, the country began to open doors wide for foreign companies," A. V. Yablokov, deputy chairman of the

Supreme Soviet's Ecological Committee, told an international congress in Gothenburg last year. "Now the people in my country are beginning to understand that penetration of foreign firms and enterprises to the USSR is connected with some dangers. Some people claim, and not without grounds, that many firms would like to develop their 'dirty' industries in our territory, such as ammoniac or pesticide productions."

"In a number of cases it occurred that Western chemical technology does not work in our land as it was pictured by advertisements, and chemical plants built according to Western projects proved to be sources of dangerous pollution of big regions, for instance near the northern coast of the Caspian Sea (the Astrakhan gas condensate complex). A public campaign has developed now against construction of a tremendous oil-gas-chemical industrial complex in western Siberia. The construction had involved American and Japanese firms."

Expanding tourism can also be a problem. Leningrad is joining forces with the Cyrus Eaton Company to construct a hotel and entertainment complex northwest of the city. The site proposed for the complex sits atop an underground water reservoir which is a secondary source of drinking water for the dreadfully polluted Leningrad (St. Petersburg) water supply. If Eaton builds the hotel, that water source will be permanently lost. In Leningrad, feeling against the project is so intense that 95 percent of the populace has come out in opposition.

Soviet Environmentalism

In the Soviet Union, as in Eastern Europe, the environment has been a rallying cry for the political undergrounds that erupted in peaceful revolution in 1989.

The Soviet environmental movement originated in the early 1960s, when individual scientists questioned Nikita Krushchev's plans to sow the "virgin lands" of western Siberia with grain, pointing to the dangers of soil erosion. In 1966, conservatives and Russian nationalists appealed to the Party Congress to save Lake Baikal, the world's largest reservoir of fresh water whose existence was threatened by unchecked logging practices and two cellulose factories built to produce cord for bomber tires. A group of noted scientists formed a committee and Andrei Sakharov took up the cause directly with Krushchev.

Then, a decade ago, a coalition of scientists protested plans to reverse the direction of rivers flowing north in Siberia and Central Asia so that they would instead spread their waters on the over-planted cotton plantations. Reestablished censorship in the late 1960s dampened the growth of the environmental movement, but what made its evolution especially difficult were the huge ministries charged with industrializing Siberia.

In today's more open political climate, saving the environment is especially important to Russian nationalists as well as to independence groups across the country.

There are five large environmental groups in the Soviet Union, the largest of which is the Socio-Ecological Union, an umbrella group with 200 branches mostly in Russia itself. The Union believes change will come through political action. The other groups include the Ecological Society of the (former) Soviet Union, which has ties with the far right *Pamyat;* the Ecological Union, which promotes solar and wind power and wants to use fines levied on polluters to clean up toxic wastes; and the All Union Movement of Greens, which was formally backed by the Communist Party's Youth organizations. People who participated in these groups often were also active in larger political organizations, such as the Popular Fronts, which were behind the rise of the reform politicians in Moscow, Leningrad and elsewhere. These reformers view environmental concerns as major issues.

Common Future

Both the United States and the Soviet Union can trace the origins of environmental pollution to the industrial revolution and the ensuing reliance on hydrocarbons. Both countries experienced horrendous pollution from coal-fired electric power plants and from projects aimed at industrializing their frontiers. These include, in the United States, diversion of the Colorado River, irrigation projects in California and the Southwest and the creation of the aluminum industry, and, in the Soviet Union, hydro-electric and water diversion schemes in Siberia and the Far East. The plans to reverse the flow of Soviet rivers is no more harebrained than former U.S. Congressman Jim Wright's notorious scheme for damming up the western trench of the Rockies in Canada and piping the water through canals into the southwestern United States. In both countries, the modern environmental movement first took shape around the issue of water pollution during the mid-1960s — Lake Baikal in the Soviet Union, and industrial pollution of the Raritan Bay, the Mississippi River and other bodies of water in the United States.

Today, the future of the environment can be tied to the often ignored race by both nations (perhaps more accurately, by corporations and ministries in both nations) to industrialize the last untrammeled part of the world in the far North. The Soviet Union exploits the Arctic in order to develop more gas for export to Europe. The United States is in search of more oil to maintain its wasteful energy system.

The Exxon Valdez spill is the most celebrated result of the race to tame the Arctic. But reports of Soviet exploitation are just as bad. For both countries, the most useful gift to future humanity would be a treaty preserving the Arctic along the lines set forth in Antarctica.

11 REVERSING THE TREND: IDEAS IN CONFLICT

NUCLEAR POWER IS A VIABLE OPTION

Frederick Bever

Frederick Bever is a Vermont-based writer on government and the environment. His article on Czechoslovakia is the result of a recent tour of Eastern Europe.

Points to Consider:

1. Why are Czechoslovakians wary of the nuclear reactors at Temelin?

2. How would nuclear power reduce air pollution?

3. What is the life expectancy in northern Bohemia?

4. Why is energy use so high in Czechoslovakia?

Excerpted from an article by Frederick Bever titled, "The Czech Challenge", appearing in **The Amicus Journal,** Spring 1990.

Uranium is our one abundant natural resource.

Many people who took to the streets in the heady November days of Czechoslovakia's peaceful, "velvet" revolution did so not only out of a desire for political and economic freedom, but because they wanted clean water to drink and clean air to breathe. Achieving these ends will be difficult, and is secondary to revamping their economy, but the Czech people have gained something unknown to them for forty years—the opportunity to share information about the environment, and to work openly and legally to improve it.

As in the rest of Eastern Europe, clean air and water are hard to come by in Czechoslovakia, where environmental degradation is pandemic and extreme. Air, water, and land have all been fouled by low-technology energy production, poorly regulated industries, and short-sighted agricultural practices.

Now, after the revolution, Czech environmentalists and their counterparts elsewhere in the Eastern bloc find themselves in the unprecedented position of setting the environmental agenda for their newly democratized countries. "During the entire period before the revolution, we could only talk about what we wanted to do—only dream," said Ivan Dejmal, a former political prisoner who now heads the environmental section of Civic Forum, the popular opposition group that orchestrated the revolution.

"Now is the chance to get something done," Dejmal added. While he says he is still an environmental pessimist, Dejmal is nonetheless taking advantage of the novel political realities in his country. "We have forty years of work to catch up on," he said.

The Popular Will

As the new government sets its environmental policies, however, it is likely to be swayed by the suddenly vocal popular will, as much as by the opinions of knowledgeable men and women like Dejmal. This was made abundantly clear in the middle of January, when energy minister Frantisek Pinc announced the suspension of the Czech government's longstanding plans to construct two nuclear reactors in Temelin, a small town in rural southern Bohemia, near the Austrian border.

Two 1,000-watt reactors are nearing completion in Temelin, and the first is due to go on line in 1992. Two other, smaller reactors are already on line in the republic. Both the operating and the planned reactors use Soviet reactor technology—which

forgoes containment vessels. Although the Temelin reactors are of a more advanced design than the plant at Chernobyl, public sentiment in Czechoslovakia is heavily against the use of Soviet technology.

The plans for the two new reactors were quickly targeted for neutralization by anti-nuclear activists in Czechoslovakia and Austria, once the Communist regime fell. Pinc complained—while carefully voicing his respect for free speech—that anti-Temelin demonstrations had dogged his steps in the days before his decision to suspend construction of the reactors. On the two reactors already on line, Pinc refused to take any action, beyond promising a study on reducing their power output.

With Chernobyl fresh in its mind, the public is extremely fearful of nuclear power. But to Pinc, and many environmental scientists as well, there is a far graver danger to the health of the Czech people and their environment: airborne toxins.

Approximately thirty coal-firing plants supply nearly 60 percent of the country's energy. Burned in decades-old furnaces—both residential and industrial—with little or no pollution-control technology, the low quality "brown" coal produces sulfur dioxide and nitrous oxide, which combine in the air to create acid rain of a virulency unknown in the United States, and rivaled on the European continent only in Poland.

The acrid stench of poorly burned coal pervades the air in Czechoslovakia. Prague's countless statues and monuments are blackened with soot, their features eroded by acid fallout. As much as 70 percent of the forests throughout the countryside are estimated to be in decline, due in part to acid rain.

In northern Bohemia, which abounds with energy intensive industries, concentrations of airborne sulfur dioxide exceed the government's own health standards fully one-third of the year, sometimes by several factors of ten. Jan Jecminek, a doctor and the spokesman for the burgeoning Green Party of northern Bohemia, flatly states that many of the cancers and respiratory diseases he has treated are attributable to air pollution. "The illnesses of civilization, which are decreasing in other countries, are increasing in ours," Jecminek said. "We won't live as long as you." At sixty-seven years, the average life expectancy in Czechoslovakia is one of the lowest in Europe. In northern Bohemia, the average life expectancy is only fifty-four years.

Nuclear Option

Jecminek is opposed to the Temelin project. But like most of the environmentalists, scientists, politicians, and bureaucrats interviewed for this article, he sees nuclear power as a partial solution to air pollution. "Temelin is being built in an ecologically sensitive area," Jecminek said. "This is virgin countryside, with few protected reserves, and rare vegetation. The moment they start building the reactors, there will be a reason to start new industrial enterprises around Temelin, to use its energy. If they built a nuclear power station in northern Bohemia — using French technology, not Russian — then the energy could be used without having to transfer it long distances, and southern Bohemia would remain pristine."

Dejmal has a similar point of view. "Uranium is our one abundant natural resource," he said. "If we accept the view that nuclear power is inevitable, we must make sure not to support reactors as big as the Temelin project, and to scatter them around the country."

But he also emphasized the need to reduce power consumption. "Our coal supply will run out in twenty years," he noted. "What will we do after that? Our republic is too far north to use solar power, so the only solution is to completely change our life-style and reduce the consumption of energy."

"We would like to find ourselves in a situation where we not only develop electric energy, but where we have modernized the gadgets that consume this energy."

Scientist Jaroslav Stoklasa, who penned the definitive study of the Czech environment, *Nature in Danger: Biosphere, Man and Technology,* with the newly installed environment minister, said that energy consumption in Czechoslovakia is 30 percent higher than in the rest of the world, relative to national income. Stoklasa attributes the country's excessive energy use to Czechoslovakia's "unfavorable" economic structure, which has been built on government controlled, low-technology production of heavy machinery and metals processing.

In the new political climate, environmentalists and energy experts are looking to the free-market economy as their best hope. Their theory is that when industrial enterprises are no longer subsidized, there will be a new and strong economic incentive to reduce energy costs.

Proposals

Stoklasa proposes four steps to achieve a sustainable ecology under rapid economic expansion. First, market-based prices should be applied to the energy and raw materials used by both public and industrial consumers. Stoklasa acknowledges that consumers will not easily adjust to paying market prices for energy, and that this could destabilize the new government. "Mr. Havel may not be so popular then," Stoklasa said.

Second, Stoklasa proposes to place a tax on the purchase of

energy, to be used by the government for research and the acquisition of pollution control technology from the West.

Third, penalties should be effectively levied on heavy polluters. Before the revolution, many penalties instituted by the national government were reduced by local municipal officials in return for favors, and it became much cheaper for the industries to pay the fines than to stop polluting.

Finally, and as a complement to the third proposal, Stoklasa envisions the creation of "pollution rights", as they have been proposed in the West and used in West Germany. Under such a system, enterprises that keep emissions below government standards are awarded the right to sell the difference to other industries.

The challenge for Czechoslovakia is clear: to integrate environmentally sensitive practices into the process of revitalizing the economy. Environmentalists recognize that the populace is hoping for a rapid increase in consumer goods at affordable prices, and that some may not care about how that goal is achieved.

12   REVERSING THE TREND:
IDEAS IN CONFLICT

NUCLEAR POWER
IS NOT A SOLUTION

Andre Carothers

Andre Carothers is the staff editor for Greenpeace Magazine. *Carothers visited the Republic of Ukraine in August of 1990.*

Points to Consider:

1. How often can we expect a major nuclear accident?

2. What happened in the first days after the Chernobyl disaster?

3. What is "Chernobyl AIDS"?

4. Why have most of the health effects of Chernobyl not yet surfaced?

Andre Carothers, "Children of Chernobyl," **Greenpeace Magazine**, January/February 1991.

The Chernobyl accident should by all rights end the centralized push for nuclear power. In Eastern Europe, where the first blush of democracy has brought environmental issues to the forefront of public concern, working reactors are being shut down and future orders shelved.

The Republic of the Ukraine, August 1990: We are winding north on a two-lane highway from Kiev toward Chernobyl and what they call the Zone—a 30-kilometer circle of highly radioactive terrain around the entombed reactor. I expect to see something amiss, some indication that this landscape and the wide swath of contaminated earth that stretches 100 miles to the northwest is the site of the most devastating industrial accident in modern history.

Fields of grain stretch to the horizon, broken by patches of green that indicate a village, or perhaps a pond. We pass through a few towns where people stare at us listlessly, no doubt unaccustomed to the sight of a van full of strangers coasting by without stopping. After an hour, I begin to feel that something is indeed wrong, something that I can't identify.

And then it comes to me. There are no children. There are few young people, in fact few people at all. The towns appear to be half empty, the remaining inhabitants mostly middle-aged or older. The only other thing that betrays the fact that this is a radiological hell is the occasional evacuated town, its main road creased by barbed wire and posted with signs—"Entry Forbidden, Radiological Danger."

Hidden are the thousands of radiation-related illnesses yet to appear, the hospital wards full of victims now suffering, the anguish of the hundreds of uprooted families. The director of nuclear safety of the International Atomic Energy Agency says that we can expect a major nuclear accident to occur roughly every 10 years. This is what it looks like in the Ukraine, year five of Chernobyl.

"If only radiation were red," said one of the few doctors who stayed to work in the Zone, "then these people would know what they are living in." More than 135,000 people have been evacuated from the area nearest the entombed reactor, but another four million live under conditions of severe radiological contamination, according to Yuri Shcherbak, chairman of the (former) Supreme Soviet's Environment Committee. Shcherbak thinks the accident may end up costing $400 billion, a figure

that exceeds both the money the country has spent building nuclear reactors and the energy generated by that investment. In other words, it would have been cheaper if Moscow had never considered using nuclear power.

First Response

In the first few days after April 16, 1986, when an experiment gone awry blew the top off the Chernobyl reactor, few realized the nature of what had happened. The Soviet nuclear power program, like much in Soviet society, was shrouded in secrecy—nothing was meant to go wrong, and anything that did was covered up. According to Zhores Medvedev, a dissident Soviet historian and nuclear expert who has written the most comprehensive assessment to date of the Chernobyl disaster, the blame rests squarely in the nature of Soviet society: at fault was the obsessive secrecy and numbing conformity that has stifled the ability of scientists and engineers to think for themselves.

Medvedev, who has cataloged a harrowing list of previously undocumented mishaps, says that nuclear authorities covered up an accident at the Leningrad Atomic Power Reactor in 1976. Had the nature of this accident been public knowledge, he insists, Chernobyl might never have occurred. Leningrad, like Chernobyl, is a graphite-moderated reactor.

Nozdrische was a bustling farm town on April 26, 1986, when Chernobyl blew up. One month later, Soviet authorities evacuated it. The houses stand open. A bundle of letters sits on a windowsill, an aging black-and-white photograph of a happy couple on their wedding day hangs askew on one wall. In one tattered parlor, the table is laid for a meal that was suddenly interrupted. A day calendar lies on the floor, the pages torn to May 24, 1986, the day Nozdrische was evacuated. Our Geiger counter rattles as we walk down the overgrown paths—four millirems per hour in the doorway, 11 on a pile of debris where a gutter channels rainfall onto the ground.

Like a child flinging a handful of wet sand, the blasted reactor scattered radiation unevenly across the Ukraine and Byelorussia. Officials evacuated some villages in the weeks after the accident but left adjacent communities behind. Just 100 yards short of the barbed wire that isolates Nozdrische, a couple lives with their 12-year-old daughter. They have tried to leave, says the father, but the government has offered only 15,000 rubles for the house. He has traveled to other parts of the Ukraine 19 times in search of a new home. But without at least 50,000 rubles, he

Dr. Vladmir Chernousenko, 50, a nuclear physicist, was scientific supervisor of the emergency team sent into Chernobyl, Ukraine, a few days after a meltdown in nuclear reactor No. 4 caused a fatal explosion on April 26, 1986.

Chernousenko believes the Chernobyl catastrophe eliminated the last hope of practical use of nuclear power, which he considers the most dangerous threat faced by the world's environment. It is impossible, he says, to build a "safe" reactor, and even if one managed such a feat — and even if man could devise safe ways to deal with the lethal waste that has been accumulating since the first atomic tests — the technology would be too expensive.

Peter Matthiessen, "Dying Victim of Chernobyl Says No Nuclear Plant Is Safe," **New York Times,** October 10, 1991.

says, the family cannot afford to move. "Perhaps a quarter of our village has already left," says his wife. "I worry most about my daughter." We poke the Geiger counter into corners of their small garden: one millirem per hour near the vegetables, more than three at a muddy spot where rainwater pours off the eaves.

Health Effects

A comprehensive assessment of the health effects of the 50 million-plus curies of radioactivity ejected from Chernobyl remains to be conducted. What information does exist is anecdotal and terrifying. According to an article in the *Times* of London, "hospitals in the Ukraine, Byelorussia and adjacent provinces are filled with victims. Whole wards are lined with gaunt, dying children." Moscow hosted an international telethon to raise money for Chernobyl relief, during which a spokesman referred to 800,000 children at risk of contracting leukemia.

Ukrainian doctors now routinely refer to what they call "Chernobyl AIDS", a radiation-caused immune deficiency that is not understood, or even accepted, by the medical community. Yet a vast array of illnesses, including pneumonia, tuberculosis, vision problems such as cataracts, anemia and other blood disorders, headaches, sleeplessness, nosebleeds and hair loss are all on the rise. Much about this disaster is new and unexpected. There has simply never been a radiological accident of this scale before. And more is yet to come. Much of the damage that radiation causes to living cells manifests itself long after the exposure — tumors and leukemia that show up after three or four years, to genetically determined disorders that appear in the next generation. "It is not like anything we deal with in terms of disasters," says Tom McDowell, the director of Union Chernobyl USA, a group formed to aid veterans of the Massive Chernobyl clean-up. "It's not like an earthquake, it's not like a flood. It keeps demanding lives and it doesn't stop in our lifetime."

Few anticipated that the Chernobyl accident would become the disaster that it is. Chernobyl was supposed to be a brief setback to the Soviet Union's and the world's inexorable march toward nuclearization. After the explosion and the initial delayed evacuation of the 45,000 residents of Pripyat, the new city built next to the reactor complex, Moscow began to speak immediately of the struggle to "eliminate the effects of the Chernobyl accident." All references to the disaster were cloaked in the terms used to describe all traumatic junctures in Soviet history: the heroic struggle of the good and selfless people against a few selfish criminals who put the great Soviet nation at risk but who are eventually revealed and vanquished. Like all such legends, a mythology about the true effects of the accident had to be manufactured, and the great cover-up began.

Not a Solution

In its most appalling manifestation, this global cover-up was demonstrated by the near absence of any significant international aid for Chernobyl's victims. After all, how many countries have had to organize international telethons along the lines of a Jerry Lewis muscular dystrophy fundraiser to pay for disaster relief? Here is a disaster of global proportions, yielding thousands of injuries and hundreds of thousands of refugees, and one is left with the chilling sense that most nations wish it would just go away.

The Chernobyl accident should by all rights end the centralized push for nuclear power. In Eastern Europe, where the first blush of democracy has brought environmental issues to the forefront of public concern, working reactors are being shut down and future orders shelved. A study by the Chernobyl Union reports that public opposition in the Soviet Union has forced the cancellation of dozens of nuclear reactors, equivalent to the country's entire current capacity.

"I went to Chernobyl two days after the explosion," says

Constantine Masyk, Deputy Prime Minister of the Ukraine. "I received 100 rems, the doctors told me." There is a hint of pride in his voice, the pride mixed with pathos and sacrifice that one hears when people speak of overcoming any one of the monumental hardships the country has faced in the last five decades. Repeating "100 rems," he holds up his hands, as if their lines would reveal the extent of the exposure, 20 times that permitted annually in the U.S. nuclear industry. Many top officials in the Soviet government risked dangerous levels of radiation to go to the stricken reactor and see the extent of the catastrophe.

Ivan Drach, like many of the new generation of Eastern European leaders, is a poet and playwright. Drach speaks passionately about Chernobyl, no doubt in part because his son, Maksym, received a massive dose of radiation as part of the first medical team that worked in the Zone. Although he is well now, Maksym could succumb to his exposure at any time.

"Nobody at the time thought it would become such a disaster. Nobody here could even envisage that it could develop into such a tragedy. The truth was hidden because officials did not want to spend the billions of rubles it will take to cure this wound."

"Chernobyl opened our eyes. For the first time we understand what sovereignty means, what democracy means, what freedom means. The Ukraine has been sacrificed. This nation, which possesses thousands of years of history, is now on its knees, its radioactive knees. This is not drama — this is tragedy. But the most important thing is the children. Without healthy children, we have no future. Please help the children of Chernobyl."

INTERPRETING EDITORIAL CARTOONS

This activity may be used as an individualized study guide for students in libraries and resource centers or as a discussion catalyst in small group and classroom discussions.

Although cartoons are usually humorous, the main intent of most political cartoonists is not to entertain. Cartoons express serious social comment about important issues. Using graphic and visual arts, the cartoonist expresses opinions and attitudes. By employing an entertaining and often light-hearted visual format, cartoonists may have as much or more impact on national and world issues as editorial and syndicated columnists.

Points to Consider:

1. Examine the cartoon in this activity.

2. How would you describe the cartoon's message?

3. Try to summarize the message in one to three sentences.

4. Does the cartoon's message support the author's point of view in any of the opinions in Chapter Three of this publication? If the answer is yes, be specific about which reading or readings and why.

13   REVERSING THE TREND: IDEAS IN CONFLICT

MORE EFFICIENT IRRIGATION WILL SAVE THE ARAL SEA

Lester R. Brown

Lester R. Brown is president of the Worldwatch Institute and was a participant in the Soviet Academy of Sciences' conference on the Aral Sea crisis in Nukus, Karakalpak.

Points to Consider:

1. Why has the fishing industry collapsed?

2. Describe salinization of the soil. Why is it a threat?

3. How can irrigation be improved?

4. How is population a factor?

Lester R. Brown, "The Aral Sea: Going, Going.", **Worldwatch**, January/February, 1991.

One of the keys to success is using underground water to supplement river water for irrigation.

From the air, the exposed floor of the Aral Sea looks like a moonscape. No plant or animal life is visible. Even in the marshy remnants of the sea, a type of wetland normally teeming with life, only an occasional pelican-like bird or wild duck emerges.

A few hundred feet above the ground, from a canvas-winged, single-engine biplane, the signs of a dying ecosystem are evident. Fishing villages that once stood by the shoreline are abandoned and lie miles from the receding waters. Like ghost mining towns out of the American West, they reinforce the image of a dying ecosystem and a dying economy.

The Aral Sea is quite literally evaporating before our eyes. Water from the Amu Darya and Syr Darya Rivers, which once emptied glacial melt from the mountains of northeastern Afghanistan and Kirghizia into this vast geologic depression in Soviet Central Asia, now irrigates surrounding cropland. The Amu Darya disappears before it reaches the Aral Sea; the Syr Darya is a mere trickle when it gets there.

The sea has dropped more than 40 feet in the last 30 years, reducing the Aral's area by 40 percent and its volume by 66 percent. Thirty miles separate some former coastal towns from the water. If recent trends continue, the sea will largely disappear within another decade or two, existing only on old maps, a geographic memory.

Fish Out of Water

Like a fish out of water, Muynak, the region's principal fish-processing center, is now stranded miles inland from the sea that was its lifeblood. In the late 1950s, the Aral yielded more than 100 million pounds of marketable fish a year, most of it headed to Muynak. Sixty thousand people worked in fishing, fish processing, and related activities in the region. By the early 1980s, though, increasing salinity had killed off 20 of the 24 commercial fish species found in the sea. As the fish disappeared, so did the fishing industry. In the early years of the sea's retreat, a canal was dug from the port across the seabed to the open water. Disappearing fish stocks underlined the futility of this effort.

Unwilling to face local political unrest, the authorities in Moscow decided to keep the processing plant going with fish brought in from the Baltic states. Traveling by refrigerated railroad car for nearly 2,000 miles; the fish finish their journey with a 60-mile truck ride from the nearest railhead. It's doubtful that this arrangement can survive the shift to a market economy.

Flying toward Muynak roughly on the course fishing boats once took to port, one witnesses perhaps the most graphic symbol of the region's economic decline: the ship cemetery. Here is the final resting place for many of the vessels that harvested the sea's rich stores of seafood. Also scattered about are the rusting hulks of ships that plied routes between coastal towns, transporting goods and people.

Salt Fallout

Only within the last few years have outsiders gained access to the Aral Sea basin, and to the data measuring its demise. Among the first to visit was Philip Micklin, a geographer at Western Michigan University in Kalamazoo. His findings appeared in a 1988 *Science* magazine article that revealed for the first time in the West the many dimensions of this unfolding environmental catastrophe. Perhaps as stark as the narrative was a satellite photograph accompanying the piece that showed a long white cloud, perhaps a third as long as the Aral Sea itself, forming on the east coastline. It was a salt storm in the making.

As the sea shrinks, it leaves behind a vast salt-covered plain incapable of supporting plant life. Each year, the wind sweeps up sand and between 90 and 140 million tons of salt in blinding storms, depositing it across a broad area. Salt from the Aral's former seabed is deposited to the northwest as far as the farms of Byelorussia and to the southeast as far as the glaciers in Afghanistan that feed the Amu Darya.

Salt fallout, whether in the form of dust or rainfall, is altering soil chemistry and affecting land productivity hundreds of miles away from the Aral. Close by, roughly half a ton of the salt/sand mix from the seabed is falling on each acre of irrigated land annually. The Soviets have the dubious distinction of adding a new phenomenon to the global litany of environmental ills: salt rain.

Land Gone Barren

One of the potential risks associated with river-diversion irrigation is that water percolating downward will gradually raise the water table. If the water table rises to within a few feet of the surface, deep-rooted crops cannot develop properly in the waterlogged soil. If it rises to within a foot or less of the surface, the underground water begins to evaporate through the soil,

GHOSTS OF THE ARAL SEA FLEET

leaving behind a layer of salt. At some point, salt accumulates to levels that are toxic to plants, at first reducing yields and eventually rendering the soil barren.

If natural drainage systems exist or if drainage is incorporated into the design of irrigation systems, this debilitating waterlogging and salinization process can be avoided. Unfortunately, in the Aral Sea basin, as in many other places, this was not the case. The same scourge that contributed to the decline of the early Mesopotamian civilizations, and today afflicts irrigated farmland in California and other arid and semi-arid regions, is claiming yet another victim.

Data from the Aral Sea basin indicate that the region may be experiencing some of the worst salinization in the world. Nikita Glazovsky, deputy director of the (former) Soviet Academy of Science's Institute of Geography, estimated that the share of irrigated land that is moderately to heavily salted ranges from 35 percent in Tajikistan to 80 percent in Turkmenistan. For the entire basin, it is 60 percent. By comparison, Mohammed El-Ashry, vice president of the World Resources Institute, reports that 25 percent of the irrigated land in California falls into this category.

Using cotton yields as an indicator, the productivity of land in the Aral region peaked in 1979. Since then, it has fallen by nearly 15 percent, despite an intensive effort to boost yields in recent years. Unless action is taken quickly to reverse this process, yields will continue to fall until eventually the land becomes sterile and is abandoned. For the 32 million people who live in the Aral Sea basin, the economic effects of environmental decline are all too obvious.

Stemming the Tide

Peter Rogers, a professor of engineering at Harvard University, sees some similarities between the situation in the Aral Sea basin today and that in Pakistan in the early 1960s. Severe waterlogging and salinity in the Indus River basin were decommissioning nearly 50,000 acres of Pakistani farmland every year. Rogers and other members of an international team designed a water management program that reversed the salinization and restored the productivity of damaged land.

One of the keys to success in Pakistan, and probably in the Aral Sea basin as well, is using underground water to supplement river water for irrigation. Shallow wells and irrigation pumps can do the job simply and inexpensively. Drawing underground water would lower the water table, reduce waterlogging and salting, and free river water to sustain the Aral Sea. In locations where underground water is too salty to be used directly for irrigation, it can be pumped into the river, where its salt content is diluted, as now occurs naturally with irrigation drainage water in parts of the basin.

Another key to freeing river water is to irrigate more efficiently. In the great haste to boost cotton production, thousands of miles of canals were dug across the land without being lined. Incalculable amounts of water seep away as a result. Aside from cutting the wasteful use of water, mandating the use of canal liners and drip irrigation systems, which are much more efficient than the furrow or flood irrigation now practiced, would lead to impressive savings.

To work, though, these methods require an incentive to save. Right now, water in the Aral Sea region is essentially free, which means that it is greatly overused, as is most any commodity when it is free or heavily subsidized.

Charging for water would lead to its more efficient use, including a shift to crops that use less water. If economic reforms progress as scheduled, the cotton production quotas will be abandoned, letting farmers decide which crops are most profitable. Differences in crop water needs can be striking. For example, it takes half as much water to produce a ton of wheat as a ton of rice. Pricing water also would likely lead to the abandonment of marginal land that uses a full share of water but yields little.

One of the few fresh proposals to emerge was offered by Y. S. Kamalov, a representative of a local grass-roots group. Kamalov suggested establishing an Aral Bank from which irrigation users would buy water. The price of water could be set so as to permit a flow of river water to at least partially restore the Aral Sea.

Proceeds from the bank could be invested in the wells and pumps needed to lower the water table and reverse waterlogging and salting. The money could also go toward teaching farmers how to use water more efficiently and to adopt pest management programs that lessen dependence on pesticides. Environmentally and economically, there is much to be said for this approach.

A Runaway Indicator

Should a strategy emerge that reverses the basin's environmental degradation and restores land productivity, it will fail to raise living standards unless population growth is slowed concurrently.

A semi-arid ecosystem with a restricted water supply cannot withstand a population growth rate of three percent per year, or twentyfold per century, for long. But leaders of the largely Muslim societies in the Aral Sea region argue that large families are a cherished tradition, something people would not give up easily.

When a population begins to outgrow its life-support systems, living standards start to fall. The 1990s may offer the last opportunity for Aral Sea republics to slow their population growth humanely, i.e., by shifting to smaller families. With the recent rise in infant mortality, cancer rates, and other forms of illness, the stage is already being set for a slowing of population growth through rising death rate. Lacking the resources to provide for a rapidly expanding population and deal with environmental threats to their people, political leaders can either actively encourage smaller families or accept the responsibility for rising death rates.

Time does not favor the Aral Sea. If those living in its basin do not soon set an agenda for the region's future, then nature will set a far grimmer one. The first step in solving the problem is recognition. This has been done. Now comes the hard part. The challenge is enormous, requiring simultaneously a restructuring of the local economy and a revolution in reproductive behavior.

14 REVERSING THE TREND: IDEAS IN CONFLICT

A RETURN TO TRADITIONAL FARMING WILL SAVE THE ARAL SEA

Bridget Morris

Bridget Morris is a Russian translator and a researcher and analyst of Soviet affairs. Her article here describes the ecological catastrophe of the Aral Sea, and how to save the area from complete destruction.

Points to Consider:

1. How fast is the Aral Sea losing its water?

2. Why are pesticides such a problem? Be specific.

3. Why has cotton not benefited the people of Central Asia?

4. What steps must be taken to revitalize the region?

Bridget Morris, "The Death of the Aral Sea", **Multinational Monitor,** September 1990.

The environmental costs of abandoning traditional farming systems for one based solely on cotton have not been offset by economic benefits for the people.

The Aral Sea represents one of the (former) Soviet Union's worst environmental catastrophes. With the Sea having shrunk to one-fifth of its former size, the fishing industry once supported by the Aral has been destroyed over the past 20 years. Much of the once-fertile land around the Sea has turned into desert and salt flats. Due to chemical pollution and erosion, the health of local people has deteriorated drastically and agricultural productivity in the region has plummeted. The birth rate is falling while infant mortality is rising. Only 38 of the 178 animal species of the region still exist.

In August 1988, a group of prominent Soviet scientists, writers, doctors, agricultural experts, hydrologists and geographers toured the Aral Sea region on the "Aral-88 Expedition". They concluded that the region is rapidly dying and will become a toxic wasteland in just a few years unless immediate action is taken to restore it.

The Roots of Destruction

The expedition members determined that the Soviet government's attempt to make the entire region a large-scale independent cotton producer is the main cause of the Aral Sea catastrophe. This effort can be traced back to 1949, when the government promoted large-scale land reclamation programs to increase agricultural productivity. At the end of the 1960s, the Ministry of Water Management (*Minvodkhoz*) of the USSR ordered the Central Asian republics to increase the water available for irrigation by taking it from the rivers, streams and other sources which normally feed into the Aral Sea. The planners did not consider the effect this might have on the Aral, even though several scientists warned that the Sea would shrink.

The *Minvodkhoz* policy resulted in the construction of thousands of kilometers of new drainage and irrigation systems, dams and water reservoirs throughout the Central Asian republics. At the same time, land used to raise livestock and to grow traditional crops, such as apricots, subtropical fruits and wheat, were planted with cotton. Thousands of tons of chemical fertilizers and pesticides were dumped onto the cotton fields to promote high yields. The *Minvodkhoz* received billions of rubles for its Central Asian cotton project, and gained an enormous vested interest in the project's continuation.

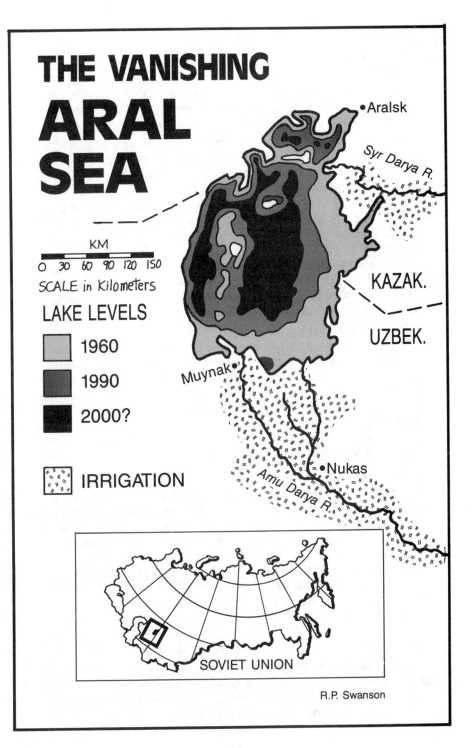

THE VANISHING
ARAL
SEA

KM
0 30 60 90 120 150
SCALE in Kilometers

LAKE LEVELS

1960
1990
2000?

IRRIGATION

•Aralsk

Syr Darya R.

KAZAK.

UZBEK.

Muynak•

•Nukas

Amu Darya R.

SOVIET UNION

R.P. Swanson

Dimensions of the Water Shortfall

From 1990 to 2000, 12-15 cubic kilometers of water are expected to flow into the Aral Sea per year. But 34-47 cubic kilometers of water evaporate from the Aral Sea each year. Consequently, the Aral is expected to lose 250 of its current 450 cubic kilometers by early in the next century.

The problem of the water siphoned from the Aral Sea is exacerbated by aging and poorly constructed irrigation and drainage systems throughout the Central Asian Republics. The drainage system malfunctions, and large amounts of water leak out. The runoff of water causes soil erosion, salinization of large areas of fertile land and waste. (The *Minvodkhoz* never even considered a water conservation policy.) Some scientists estimate that 40 percent of the water is lost from the irrigation, drainage and water reservoir systems in the Central Asian Republics. N. G. Minashin, an agricultural scientist, notes that in 1960, "4-6,000 cubic meters were used to irrigate one hectare, but now it take 10,000 cubic meters."

The Aral's shrinking has affected the local climate. The Sea contributed vital moisture and humidity to the air. The yearly evaporation of sea water into the air kept the temperature moderate most of the year and provided plenty of rainfall. As the Aral Sea shrank, the air lost its humidity and moisture. Now, the climate is much drier, and the temperature is subject to much greater variation.

Poisoned Waters

The uncontrolled use of pesticides and chemical fertilizers on the cotton fields of the Aral region has polluted and salinized the soil of the surrounding land and the sea itself. Chemicals contaminated the soil, leaked into the groundwater and were transported into rivers, lakes, streams and the Aral Sea from both runoff and the faulty irrigation and drainage systems. The result: billions of tons of poisonous salts have covered 2.6 million hectares of the Aral Sea bottom. Tens of millions of tons of salt and chemicals, many of them toxic, evaporate into the air from the Aral Sea and are spread for long distances by the wind. The salt and chemical dust has been measured 2,000 miles away in the air over Byelorussia and Latvia.

"The Aral Sea as an independent ecosystem died 13-15 years ago," states N. V. Aladin, a biologist and associate at the Zoological Institute of the Academy of Sciences of the (former) USSR. The surviving animal species are not even native to the

Aral Sea region, but were transplanted there from other parts of the Soviet Union.

Yet the spraying of chemicals and pesticides continues in many areas. The chairman of the Committee to Save the Aral Sea—the Union of the Writers of Uzbekistan, P. Shermuckhamedov, says, "Associates at the Hydrometeorological Center of Uzbekistan analyzed the composition of the water and concluded that pesticides such as B-58, metaphos, butyphos, hexachloran, lindane, DDT, and DDE are still heavily used in spite of bans. In 1988, there were 82 cases of high-level hexachloran pollution and 32 cases of lindane pollution." Many of these chemicals are found in large amounts in the major rivers, the Syr Darya and Amu Darya.

One result of the water pollution is unsafe drinking water. The amount of poisonous chemicals and salts in the water is a "murderous dose" according to A. D. Deriglazov, assistant dean at the Second Moscow Medical Institute. He says that 80 percent of the population of the Central Asian republics lacks access to clean water.

Exposure to toxic chemicals is inevitable since the chemicals sprayed on crops end up in the water and locally raised produce and meat. In the Chimkent region, for example, the meat contains eight times the maximum permissible level of pesticides, and the fruits and vegetables contain 16 times the maximum permissible level of pesticides.

Uncontrolled use of pesticides and chemicals has had a devastating effect on the health of many people in the Central Asian region. The incidence of certain diseases increases sharply in populations right around the Aral Sea. For example, residents of Aralsk, located on the edge of the Aral, suffer from typhoid and hepatitis at rates 29 times higher than the national average. Jaundice and dysentery are also prevalent in the region. Health problems are exacerbated by insufficient medical facilities. In Uzbekistan, only one out of five hospitals has running water and only three out of ten have plumbing. There is a massive shortage of hospital beds.

Children have suffered the most. The mortality rate among children less than one year of age is 98-100 per 1,000. Child mortality is higher in the Central Asian republics than in Paraguay and 20 times higher than in Japan.

Many children will not nurse at their mothers' breasts because their milk is 3-4 times saltier than the norm due to the salinization of the region, which has increased the amount of salts in food and water. Refusing to nurse, many become malnourished and sick.

The Cotton Economy

The environmental costs of abandoning traditional farming systems for one based solely on cotton have not been offset by economic benefits for the people of the region. Much of the money earned form the cotton harvests has not been reinvested in the local economy. The central government in Moscow determined how to use all funds.

Over half of the 20 million rural residents of Central Asia are involved in the cotton industry; there is almost no other type of farming left. Earnings from cotton exports are used to buy wheat, dairy products, meat and fruits—all of which were at one time abundantly available from the Central Asian republics.

While the production of cotton continues to increase, the standard of living for the average rural family continues to fall. A typical family of 7-8 earns 200-250 rubles per month, and average family incomes are decreasing. Vegetables and fruits purchased at the local markets are more expensive than those sold in Moscow. The typical Central Asian rural resident eats an average of 8 kilograms of meat per year, far below the national average of 65 kilograms per year.

Cotton dominates the society. Children and the elderly work in the fields. The children often work for long hours and miss many days of school. Local party and government members who spoke with members of the Aral-88 expedition denied that children miss school, since child labor is against the law. But local residents confirmed that it happens on a regular basis, and the expedition members frequently saw children working in the fields. In Turkmenistan, only 15.5 percent of the school-age children were in class during the cotton harvest in 1987.

Working in cotton fields is a hot and physically demanding job. Many field workers, including children and pregnant women, suffer from dehydration. Field workers are also exposed to large doses of chemical fertilizers and pesticides, leading many to contract cancer, anemia, dystrophy, allergies and jaundice.

A Bleak Future

The Aral-88 expedition members argued that the *Minvodkhoz* program (of water diversion) would waste 55-60 billion rubles while furthering the environmental destruction of the Aral. They said the Aral Sea and the surrounding area need immediate emergency aid. They proposed three steps to gradually revitalize the region. First, water used for irrigation of cotton fields should be reduced by 20 percent, allowing more water to flow into the Aral Sea, and water should be rationed.

Second, the Aral-88 expedition members called for the reinstatement of traditional farming and an end to the cotton monopoly in the region. Cotton is a very thirsty crop; it has not been profitable or beneficial for the Soviet Union, and certainly not for the residents of Central Asia.

The third and most controversial step would be to restore the original plant life to the defoliated Aral Sea bottom.

The expedition members also called for the government to take steps to restore and protect the health of the Central Asian people. They said it should launch a campaign to prevent people from drinking the local water and should ship bottled water into the region for popular consumption. The government will need to invest billions in building better medical facilities and in providing more physicians and uncontaminated food products. The Aral-88 members said their proposal should be considered an emergency aid program, and noted that the Aral Sea catastrophe may cost much more than the Chernobyl disaster.

15   REVERSING THE TREND:
IDEAS IN CONFLICT

GLOBAL ENVIRONMENTALISM
IS THE ANSWER

Dick Russell

Dick Russell is a contributing editor to the Amicus Journal. *This article deals with the "green" movement in the (former) Soviet Union.*

Points to Consider:

1. Who are the SEU and *Goskompriroda*?

2. What progress have ecology groups made in the (former) Soviet Union?

3. How did the (former) Soviet government responded to environmental problems?

4. Why are ecological concerns often overshadowed in the (former) Soviet Republics?

Excerpted from article by Dick Russell titled, "Comrades Unite!" **The Amicus Journal,** Summer 1991.

By far the best course of action would be "planetary management", where nations might cooperate on projects designed to minimize environmental destruction.

Nearly everyone has heard about the meltdown at Chernobyl. Few Americans, however, have heard of Chelyabinsk, a nuclear materials factory where continuing releases of nuclear waste since 1957 have created one of the most polluted spots in the world. Or of Ufa, a city just west of the Urals, where industrial chemicals were accidentally dumped into the water supply last year; for several weeks, until local authorities reported the accident, residents drank water with dioxin levels exceeding the Soviet health standard by 147,000 times. Who has heard about the babies of Karakalpakia born alongside the Amu Darya river, which one resident calls "the sewer of central Asia"."Infant mortality in the region is extremely high at sixty deaths per 1,000 live births.

These are just a few of the environmental catastrophes, largely unknown to the outside world, that have led to an explosion of environmental activism across the (former) Soviet Union. In the wake of *perestroika*, hundreds, possibly thousands, of environmental groups have formed over the past five years. "Green activism is in the vanguard of democratization throughout the former USSR," Eric Green, author of *Ecology and Perestroika,* has noted. But, amid the economic upheaval and rampant nationalism in this vast region, lately there have come signs of retrenchment on ecological progress by the Russian government.

Eco-Conference

Gorbachev's reversal on some progressive environmental policies and the stories like those of Chelyabinsk and Ufa were the central themes of a remarkable six-day gathering in March 1991 on the outskirts of Moscow. It was the first non-governmental conference on the environment ever held between the USSR and the United States. About fifty Americans, representing the National Resource Defense Council (NRDC), the Sierra Club, Audubon Society, Earth Island Institute, Work on Waste, Center for Clean Air Policy, and other organizations, came together with their counterparts from more than 100 Soviet environmental groups.

The Soviet effort was organized by the Socio-Ecological Union

(SEU), an umbrella organization linking more than 150 grassroots groups across the (former) USSR, with the tacit approval of *Goskompriroda,* the Soviet agency equivalent to the U.S. Environmental Protection Agency (EPA). Soviet participation exceeded expectations, in part because no political obstacles intervened, and many of the Soviets, who hailed from regions as far as ten time zones apart, were meeting each other for the first time.

A Matter of Survival

For the Soviet people, environmentalism is not a quality-of-life issue, as it often is in the United States. In this vast area where the excesses of industrialization have all but swallowed entire ecosystems, environmentalism is quite starkly a matter of survival. In 1987, the health costs of pollution in this (former) nation were estimated at about 11 percent of the GNP, or the equivalent of $330 billion.

Before Gorbachev, statistics such as these were closely guarded, and dissent about governmental actions, as expressed at the Moscow conference, was unheard of. In the last few years, the environmental movement has found its voice and has made substantial strides. Its outcry shut down three chemical plants in Armenia. In the Ukrainian city of Odessa, the Green Party candidate defeated the *oblast* [province] party boss in elections to the local soviet, and a number of cooperatives are providing solid financial backing for Green activities. These are but two of numerous examples.

Yet the challenges facing groups like the Azerbadzhani Greens or the Ecological Movement of Tomsk are daunting. Who is responsible for pollution? What do you do about strict but ignored and unenforced pollution control laws? Who makes decisions about a plant causing tremendous pollution in Azerbadzhan while making products primarily for use in Armenia? How can you close a plant emitting toxic fumes if it is producing crucial medical supplies? How can you not close it?

As the former Soviet environmentalists told it—and their ability to speak frankly remains an astonishing outcome of the Gorbachev era—the government's response to those questions has become woefully intractable.

Svetlana Revina, a scientist who also serves on the Russian Federation's Ecological Commission, summed up the ineptness of *Goskompriroda:* "Seventy percent of its employees are not professionals but people from the apparatus [bureaucracy] who had been fired. [They have] no care for the environment."

We Prefer Bread

One gray morning during the conference, the Soviet organizers drove a busload of Americans to Bitsa, a small settlement just south of Moscow. A citizens' movement had arisen here to try to stop 150,000 housing units from being built right through the middle of a forest belt. They had persuaded the Moscow City Council to hold off on a new highway, the first stage of the project. Soon after, the houses of two of the movement's leaders burned to the ground; the Americans viewed the charred remains. Questions hung over the gathering: did the authorities do it, or was it Bitsa residents themselves, acting in the belief that they would be deprived of what the Party had promised, modern apartments for an area where water must be carried from street-corner pumps?

There lies the rub about environmentalism in the (former) USSR. As the questions raised at Bitsa illustrate, there seems to be a national conflict between fulfilling basic needs such as running water, and protecting the environment. One activist described the typical reaction to her environmentalism: "If we did not have these factories, we would be refugees." And as Moscow economist Vasily Sokolov said privately, "Sometimes we prefer bread to be a little polluted rather than have nothing on the table."

Putting food on the table is an immediate concern for most Soviets; creeping ecological decay is, unfortunately, far less tangible. "You can't save the environment under the present system," the conference's chief SEU organizer, Maria Cherkasova, said flatly. "In the past, we had direct and open genocide, prison camps. Now there are more and more places where human beings just can't live. [This country is] a gas chamber under an open sky."

Planetary Approach

Everywhere you look in society there are the effects of decades of apathy about ecological problems. The average lifespan of the Siberian coal miner is fifty-seven years; at the last call-up of young men for the military draft, fully one-half did not qualify to serve for reasons of health.

Where, amidst such dilemmas, is there room for assistance from the American environmental movement? The answer is not as hopeless as it might appear. The conference organizers' goal was not just simply informational exchange, but to have this international meeting mark the beginning of a series of tangible,

THE GREEN CURTAIN

Nature must be protected—for her own sake—from the uninhibited expansion of people. Only in this way can she remain the basis for human community and culture. Before undertaking any and every economic activity we have to ask: where is it going? for whom? why?

The Green Party (formed in East Germany in 1989) supports principally a sustainable development. We want to prevent the present reform movement in our country from building a self-advancing society of waste and disposable mentality under the pressure of an unreasonable, short-sighted, materialistic need to catch up with the West.

Katrin Zielke, "The Green Curtain," **Mother Jones**, April/May 1990.

long-term collaborative projects between East and West.

"It is precisely because the system here is so much in transition that you find some opportunities that wouldn't otherwise exist," said EPA's Bill Freeman. "They are introducing an economic mechanism for environmental protection, involving more realistic resource pricing, greatly increased charges for pollution, and the creation of earmarked funds especially for environmental concerns." He said he hopes that both EPA and private U.S. environmental groups will be able to lend expertise.

In the future, we are likely to see greater pressure from U.S. environmentalists on multinational corporations that are setting up shop in the (former) Soviet Union. Chevron, for instance, has negotiated a joint oil and gas venture near the Caspian Sea. The drilling will begin in a flood zone, threatening the region's already vastly depleted populations of salmon and sturgeon, said Svet Zebelin of the SEU.

By the far the best course of action would be "planetary management", said economist Solokov, where nations might cooperate on projects that are designed to minimize environmental destruction. He suggested that Japan and the United States might invest in Siberian natural gas reserves, for example, which could then be sold to China, as an alternative to increasing Russian production of highly polluting coal.

The most important step, conference goers decided, was to create a better method for East-West communication. Soviet environmentalists remain hungry for information, sorely lacking methods of monitoring the effects of pollution, and the effects of radioactivity, and hazardous wastes. "Current efforts to cooperate are plagued by poor telephone lines, an erratic postal system, lack of equipment, and some level of continued government censorship of mail and other correspondence," according to the (former) Institute for Soviet-American Relations.

A number of joint projects have emerged from the gathering. Baikal Watch, based in San Francisco, will expand its efforts to have the Siberian lake declared a World Heritage Area by UNESCO. Plans are in the works for exchanges between farmers from the Black Sea and organic growers in New York State. And the Sierra Club will help establish a national park in the Pamir Mountains.

Paul Connett, a professor at New York's St. Lawrence University and founder of the organization Work on Waste, said it best: "I felt we were looking in many ways at a mirror image of our own society, both in terms of bureaucrats with lack of vision, and fight-back from citizens."

The historic meeting in Moscow was the explicit recognition by two superpowers that they must empower their most informed and dedicated critics.

16 REVERSING THE TREND: IDEAS IN CONFLICT

WORLD SOCIALISM IS THE ANSWER

Doug Jenness

The following comments were excerpted from an article by Doug Jenness in the Militant. *The author claims capitalism must be abolished before environmental destruction can be stopped.*

Points to Consider:

1. How is environmental damage in Eastern Europe and the (former) Soviet Union described?

2. Why is overturning capitalism not a guarantee that the environment will be protected?

3. How extensive was pollution in Bulgaria?

4. What relationship exists between communism and the environment?

Doug Jenness, "World Socialism Is the Answer", **The Militant,** August 31, 1990.

In a country where capitalist property relations have been overturned, the fight to clean up the environment will not happen automatically any more than eliminating racism will. It is connected to the same conscious effort that is needed to move toward communist society.

Large areas of Eastern Europe and the Soviet Union are plagued by the spread of poisonous gases and toxic dust as the result of industrial pollution. Tens of millions of people live and work in hazardous conditions. This is the story that is now coming out in the wake of the massive upheavals that have toppled most of the Communist Party-dominated regimes in the region.

Throughout the coal-mining areas and the industrial towns of Eastern Europe, the scope of the environmental disaster is staggering. Poland's pollution is considered the worst. The Polish Academy of Sciences today says a third of the population live in "areas of ecological disaster". The toll is heavy as cases of cancer, heart disease, emphysema, and child illnesses have sharply risen.

In Bulgaria, a Communist Party report says that about 60 percent of the land is now damaged as a result of industrial fallout and extensive use of pesticides and other chemicals.

Moreover, the people of Eastern Europe and the (former) Soviet Union are haunted by the disastrous explosion at the Chernobyl nuclear reactor in the Ukraine. This was by far the most severe nuclear accident that has yet occurred, and the contamination of air and soil continue to be a deadly threat to tens of thousands of residents.

Ending Capitalism

Do these environmental horrors mean that overturning capitalistic rule, nationalizing basic industry, and establishing planned economies won't bring an end to ecological destruction?

The facts clearly show that overturning capitalism and expropriating the capitalist class are not sufficient to reverse the degradation of our environment. They are a prerequisite, however, to accomplishing this. The profit drive of the capitalists inevitably leads to sapping the original sources of all wealth—labor and nature.

Working people can, through struggle, bring considerable

NEEDLESS WASTE

Capitalist, or demand-constrained economies, waste resources through advertising, packaging, style changes, model changes, product differentiation, product obsolescence, and credit buying which keeps the system afloat. This needlessly wastes resources and pollutes the environment. Socialist economies are much less guilty in this respect.

James O'Connor, **Z Magazine**, June 1989.

pressure to bear on the employing class to institute more anti-pollution controls and safety measures. But as long as the capitalist profit system continues to exist, all advances by working people are continually under attack and are insecure and liable to be reversed. The anarchy and destructiveness of the capitalist system has to be destroyed before a serious effort can be started to clean up the mess left by the profiteers and before new steps are made to protect the environment. Safeguarding the environment is totally intertwined with the struggle of workers and farmers to overturn capitalism.

The end of capitalism eliminates the business cycle and gets rid of distribution according to the blind laws of the market. For the first time in human history it becomes possible to consciously organize and plan the economy on the basis of the needs of the great majority.

The social produce can be apportioned so that substantially more funds can be used for rehabilitating the environment and for installing machinery and processes that are not polluting, or are far less so.

In his book *Che Guevara: Economics and Politics in the Transition of Socialism,* Cuban writer Carlos Tablada noted that Guevara's view was, "The effectiveness of the plan can't be evaluated *solely* by whether or not it improves economic management and, therefore, augments the goods available to society. Nor can it be evaluated by the earnings obtained in the production process.

"The real measure of the plan's effectiveness," he said, "lies in its potential to improve economic management in terms of advancing toward the central objective: communist society. In other words, the true gauge lies in the plan's ability to combine what is rational socially with what is rational economically."

This is the opposite of the policy carried out by the Stalinist bureaucratic castes in Eastern Europe and the Soviet Union. Their maxim was to subordinate everything to "economic growth" and "industrial development" while they skimmed off a huge chunk of the social product for themselves. They drove working people in the city and country out of political life and despoiled the environment through bureaucratic mismanagement.

The Transition

But the transition to the communist society can only come through conscious effort, through the activity of socially and politically conscious men and women. Economic decisions have to be made in conjunction with steps that will reduce social inequalities, get rid of discriminatory policies based on race and sex, and protect and upgrade the health and safety of working people and the environment.

In a country where capitalist property relations have been overturned, the fight to clean up the environment will not happen automatically any more than eliminating racism will. It is connected to the same conscious effort that is needed to move toward communist society.

The most uncompromising and politically conscious fighters for protecting the environment will become part of the communist movement, both in capitalist countries and in those countries where state property relations exist.

UNDERSTANDING MAPS

Maps can provide us with a graphic understanding of the political and social issues facing our world today. The purpose of this activity is to familiarize the reader with geographic locations and the extent of the eco-crisis in Eastern Europe and the former Soviet Union.

Guidelines

1. Refer to the map on pages 12 & 13. Listed at the lower left are the 15 republics of the (former) USSR, now struggling with their newfound independence. Using a world atlas or globe, identify the location of each republic by writing the appropriate number (1-15) before each name. You will note that one republic comprises most of the territory (no. 15) and that number appears in several locations.

2. Study the map of the Chernobyl disaster on page 34. Make a list of the Soviet Republics and the European nations that were victims of the initial radioactive fallout.

3. Once considered Europe's most beautiful river, the Danube today has become one of its most threatened. Referring to the map of Eastern Europe on page 45, list all of the nations that share the Danube River. (Not shown on the map is former West Germany where the river begins.)

4. What body of water does the Danube empty into?

5. Study the map of the Aral Sea on page 113. The fishing communities of Aralsk and Muynak used to be on the shores of the Aral Sea. Using the map scale, how far is Muynak from the water today? How far will it be by the year 2000?

BIBLIOGRAPHY

SOVIET UNION

Bangs, R. Rapid changes. *Sierra,* v. 75, May/June 1990: p. 56-61.

Brower, D. R. "Expertise 90" inspires Baikal Watch. *Earth Island Journal,* Fall 1990: p. 15.

Cherkesova, M. V. The state of Soviet Ecology. *Multinational Monitor,* March 1990: p. 23-25.

Cockburn, A. Whose better nature? Socialism, capitalism and the environment. *Z Magazine,* June 1989.

Coogan, K. Specter of Dying Aral Sea haunts USSR. *Guardian,* Fall 1990: p. 15.

Crane, K. Hot times in Siberia. *Discover,* v. 11, Dec. 1990: p. 12.

Ellis, W. S. The Aral: A Soviet sea lies dying. *National Geographic,* Feb. 1990: p. 73-92.

Fagan, S. Target Novaya Zemlya: Journey into the Soviet nuclear testing zone. *Greenpeace,* Jan/Feb 1991: p. 13-16.

Finney, B. R. The USSR-Global forum on the environment, *The Mother Earth News,* v. 122, Mar/Apr 1990: p. 60.

Garelik, G. The Soviets clean up their act. *Time,* v. 135, Jan. 29, 1990: p. 64.

Kotlyakov, V. M. The Aral Sea basin. *Environment,* v. 33, Jan/Feb 1991: p. 2-9.

Loukjanenko, V. Water crisis in the USSR. *World Health,* Jan/Feb 1990: p. 24-25.

Matthiessen, P. The blue pearl of Siberia. *The New York Review of Books,* v. 38, Feb. 14, 1991: p. 37-47.

Remnick, D. Polluted, outmoded Soviet steel town must pick its poison. *Washington Post,* May 24, 1991.

Richman, B. The changing face of environmentalism in the Soviet Union. *Environment,* v. 32, March 1990: p. 4-9.

Sakharov, A. D. Who murdered Lake Baikal? *Time,* v. 135, May 21, 1990: p. 55.

Sander, G. F. No friends to the fir. *Sierra,* v. 76, May/June 1991: p. 36-39.

Schoenfeld, G. Rad storm rising. *The Atlantic*, v. 266, Dec. 1990: p. 44.

Smith, G. The post-coup environment: What lies ahead? *Earth Island Journal*, v. 6, Fall 1991: p. 33.

Trimble, J. Heart of darkness. *U.S. News and World Report*, v. 108, June 4, 1990: p. 27-30.

Vesilind, P. J. The Baltic: arena of power. *National Geographic*, v. 175, May 1989: p. 602-35.

CHERNOBYL

Bogert, C. Chernobyl's legacy. *Newsweek*, v. 115, May 7, 1990: p. 30-31.

Castro, J. Who knows how many will die? *Time*, v. 137, Apr. 29, 1991: p. 64.

Chernobyl Fallout. *U.S. News and World Report*, v. 110, June 3, 1991: p. 17.

Chow-Bush, V. The bitter legacy of Chernobyl. *Scholastic Update*, v. 123, Apr. 19, 1991: p. 23.

Lerager, J. Voices from Chernobyl. *Earth Island Journal*, Spring 1991: p. 25.

Maysles, D. R. Revelations of a Chernobyl insider. *The Bulletin of the Atomic Scientists*, v. 46, Dec. 1990: p. 16-21.

Medvedev, Grigori. The truth about Chernobyl. *Harper Collins Publishers, Inc.* 1991.

Nemeth, M. A breath of fresh air. *Macleans*, v. 104, Aug. 26, 1991: p. 12.

Olga Korbut's deadly foe, *Peoples Weekly*, v. 35, Mar. 4, 1991: p. 34-39.

Pekkanen, J. The man who fell into hell. *Reader's Digest*, v. 138, May 1991: p. 176-80.

Sakharov, A. D. Mankind cannot do without nuclear power. *Time*, v. 135, May 21, 1990: p. 60.

Stetson, M. Chernobyl's deadly legacy revealed. *Worldwatch*, Nov/Dec 1990: p. 9-10.

Toufexis, A. Legacy of a disaster. *Time*, v. 135, Apr. 9, 1990: p. 68-70.

Underwood, N. A disaster's deadly legacy. *Macleans*, v. 104, May 13, 1991: p. 55.

What Chernobyl did. *The Economist,* Apr. 27, 1991: p. 19-21.

EASTERN EUROPE

Arp, H. Environmental policy cooperation between East and West Europe. *Environment,* v. 33, Jul/Aug 1991: p. 44-45.

Benedict, C. Dirty Germany. *Buzzworm,* v. 3, Mar/Apr 1991: p. 30-35.

Bingham, S. Cian landscapes. *Audubon,* v. 93, Jan. 1991: p. 92-103.

Charles, D. East German environment comes into the light. *Science,* v. 247, Jan. 19, 1990: p. 274-6.

Chelminski, R. The not-so-blue Danube. *Smithsonian,* v. 21, July 1990: p. 32-40.

Cherfas, J. East Germany struggles to clean its air and water. *Science,* v. 248, Apr 20, 1990: p. 295-6.

Fuhrman, P. Breathing the Polish air. *Forbes,* v. 147, June 24, 1991: p. 40-42.

Gergen, D. Cleaning up the fouled worker's paradise. *U.S. News and World Report,* v. 108, Apr. 30, 1990: p. 27.

Hamilton, J. M. Will pollution kill the revolution? *The Bulletin of the Atomic Scientists,* v. 47, June 1991: p. 12-18.

Hansen, S. Dumping toxins on the Eastern Bloc. *Multinational Monitor,* Nov. 1990: p. 6.

Hayes, D. East Europe's nuclear window. *The Nation,* v. 253, Aug. 26, 1991: p. 222-5.

Husarska, A. The pearl of Poland. *Conde Nast Traveler,* v. 26, Aug. 1991: p. 64-67.

Jensen, H. The cost of neglect. *Macleans,* v. 103, May 7, 1990: p. 54-55.

Maremont, M. East Europe's big cleanup. *Business Week,* Mar. 19, 1990: p. 114-5.

Miller, M. S. A green wind hits the east. *Technology Review,* v. 93, Oct. 1990: p. 52-63.

Painton, F. Where the skies stay dark. *Time,* v. 135, May 28, 1990: p. 40.

Schwartz, J. Cleaning up by cleaning up. *Newsweek,* v. 115, June 11, 1990: p. 40-41.

Strauss, C. The Little Red Province. *New Internationalist,* Nov. 1990: p. 14-15.

Thompson, J. Eastern Europe's dark dawn. *National Geographic,* v. 179, June 1991: p. 36-63.

Vargha, J. Incentives for new thinking. *Technology Review,* v. 93, Oct. 1990: p. 60-63.

Vorholz, F. Germany confronts "super-poison". *World Press Review,* v. 37, Dec. 1990: p. 63.

Wallich, P. Dark days. *Scientific American,* v. 263, Aug. 1990: p. 16.

Waters, R. A new dawn in Bohemia. *Sierra,* v. 75, May/June 1990: p. 34-36.

Waters, T. Ecoglastnost. *Discover,* v. 11, April 1990: p. 50-53.

APPENDIX

For further information on environmental conditions in Eastern Europe and the former Soviet Union, contact the following sources:

ISTER (East European Environmental Research)
Frankel Leout 102-104.IV.40
1023 Budapest
Hungary

Friends of the Earth
218 D St., SE.
Washington, DC 20003

Greenpeace
1436 U. Street NW.
Washington, DC 20009

Conservation International
1015 18th St., NW, Suite 1000
Washington, DC 20036

Foundation to Protect the Hungarian Environment (FPHE)
84 Old North Stamford Road
Stamford, CT 06905

SZOPK, Gorkeho
6.811 01 Bratislava
Czechoslovakia

Baikal Watch
Earth Island Institute
300 Broadway, Suite 28
San Francisco, CA 94133

Umweltant der Stadt Freiburg
Dr. Dieter Worner
Technisches, Rathans Fehrenboechallee
D-7800 Frieburg
Germany

Across Frontiers
P.O. Box 2382
Berkeley, CA 94702